Life is too Short to Wear Beige

STORIES OF LIFE, LAUGHTER, AND LOVE

by MARY MARGARET LAMBERT

2018

Life is too Short to Wear Beige

Copyright © 2016 Mary Margaret Lambert

Printed in the United States of America

First Edition

Acknowledgment

This book has been on my bucket list for many years, but each time I thought I could make it a reality, life got in the way. Perhaps God just wasn't ready for it to be done until now. Trusting in His timing, I acknowledge those who have helped to bring this to fruition.

The title originated from when our first son got married. The mother of the bride called to introduce herself to me. "Mrs. Lambert," she began. I stopped her before she could say another word. "I'm not Mrs. Lambert, I am Mary Margaret. I have been told that as the mother of the prospective groom, I am supposed to wear beige and keep my mouth shut. Sorry to tell you, but I don't do either. Now that is out of the way, I'm sure we will get along just fine." And we did, and I wore lavender and danced the night away at the reception.

My deep gratitude to my freshman English teacher in high school, Sister Amora, R.S.M. (now Margaret Longhill), who encouraged me to write and gave me confidence in my abilities. To my wonderful grandparents, Joe and Mary Catherine St. Charles Formosa, and Ewing and Margaret Ellen Curley Hurt, who made me believe that I could do anything I set my mind to and who were my life coaches and cheering squad. I proudly bear the names of both of my grandmothers. To my parents, Joe and Martha Hurt Formosa, who gave me the gift of life, love, and the opportunity for a wonderful education. To my brother Jody for his eternal sense of humor and for shared memories. To my husband, Eddie, who understood my passion for writing and supported my desire to make my dreams come true. To my children, Ed, Chuck, and Nick; to Michele, Sonya and Leslie, who enriched our family with each of their individual personalities and talents and joined forces with me to balance out our male dominated clan; my grandchildren, Sarah, Emma, Matthew, Dominic, and Nolan, who give me immeasurable joy and an unending source of inspiration and ideas. To my extended family and friends, living and deceased, who have loved and encouraged me though life's challenges and triumphs. Their names and legacies are etched forever on my heart. To Monsignor Owen Campion, who offered me the job as a columnist for the *Tennessee Register* and has been my friend for more than 60 years. To Bill Connolly and Sarah Lambert for their expertise and work in converting my articles into computer files, and to Sarah Lambert, Wendy Hodgin and Nolan Lambert for their book illustrations. To Debbie Lane for her time and talent in creating this book, to Andy Telli, my paisano editor for his keen eye and sharpened red pencil, and to my past and present editors at the *Tennessee Register,* Msgr. Campion, Anthony Spence and Rick Musacchio..

God blessed me with a wonderful talent, and I have tried to use it to inspire, amuse and inform my readers.

To Eddie My Love,
forever and always.

Chapter One: ANIMAL KINGDOM

Chapter two: ANGELS AND SAINTS

Chapter three: FAMILY MATTERS

Chapter 10: TAKE TWO ASPIRIN AND PLEASE DON'T CALL ME IN THE MORNING

Chapter 11: RAINBOWS AND LOLLIPOPS

Chapter 12: FINAL SUNSETS

ANIMAL KINGDOM

Chapter

St. Francis And His Friends

I suppose everyone has a favorite saint, perhaps more than one in some cases. Needing all the help 1 can get, I ask heavenly intervention from several, but seem to be drawn to St. Francis of Assisi. Our firstborn son, whom we lost at birth, was baptized Edward Francis in honor of his father and my favorite saint.

In our back yard, there is a statue of St. Francis because of our shared love of animals. I feel very strongly there is some kind of message emitting from the statue into the animal kingdom, just as the majestic "lady" in the New York harbor symbolizes our precious liberty and freedom. An awful lot of God's little critters must look upon our St. Francis as a symbol for room and board for all of their lame, prolific, ugly, and homeless, who long for free puppy chow, vet bills, and guaranteed adoption for all offspring.

We have, over the past 26 years, acquired the most interesting array of animals imaginable. (I once called the Internal Revenue Service to see if our vet bills were tax deductible.) Ranging from the parakeet we had who walked upside down in his cage, the pony who escaped under fences, the ducks who chased dogs, and enough black mollies to equal the number of Imelda Marcos' shoes, there have been some really memorable pets. When my oldest son bought his girlfriend a rabbit, while they were away at college, he, of course, got summer custody. When the aroma of warm bunny became less than desirable in the laundry room, I decided it was time for it to live with its mother. I was severely chastised for this action, as it lost a race with a German Shepherd soon after moving away.

We have had five little "wiener" dogs. We tend to favor dachshunds because of their gentle nature and good disposition around children. They, unfortunately, are also very neurotic and become quickly and easily spoiled. Our "Freida," the neighborhood gossip, was 14 years old when she, frightened by Fourth of July fireworks, became confused and wandered away, never to be seen again. To ease my grief over losing her, we accepted a foster "doxie" named "Willie," an abandoned puppy whose first family had to give him up. He has been with us for five years now, and aside from eating entire blocks of cheese intended for dinner guests, and rolling up, cocoon style, in a blanket every night, he's fairly well adjusted. He has a sister, "Pepper," the runt of my brother's litter of mixed peek-a-poos. She has a lame back leg and a steel pin in her front appendage, but manages to keep pace with our newest addition, "Hank." Now this dog is the coup-de-grace of all our pet acquisitions. Here, just when we thought life began at 40, (or thereabouts), we have a very large, affectionate, hungry, and less than beautiful canine to care for, and love. He was a graduation "gift" to our youngest son from "friends"(?). We protested vehemently, but with a 17-year -old swearing to accept total responsibility for him, how could we feel uneasy?

We got him in May, selecting April Fools Day as a most appropriate birth-day for him, and were awarded sole custody when college began in September. He has found it difficult to remain confined in our fenced back yard, as he was bred to tend cattle. Since the neighbors would probably frown upon us having cows to occupy him, we have spent the last few months attempting to thwart all of his escape attempts.

He loves to torment our aged cat, "Friday," who at 18 is very nearsighted, a bit deaf, and not very agile anymore. Since I am allergic to cats, and this is most probably the reason for her longevity, it is a constant challenge to keep her out of the house, and away from his rowdy chases. She also has a weak bladder, and tends to mark her possessions in a highly personal manner. This can be attested to by a very dear and understanding friend, who is now the owner of a strangely odorous rabbit coat.

Lest I seem ungrateful, be assured that I am ever thankful that my life has been blessed with each and every one of these little — and big — creatures. In silent communication, all have taught me, and mine, about the wonders of God's love and beauty in the world. St. Francis will always remain in a most prominent part of my garden, and in my heart.

THERE ONCE WAS A PUPPY NAMED PEPPER

*T*here once was a puppy named Pepper.

Ten years ago this spring, my brother and sister-in-law offered us a pup from their "Spooky's" litter. At first we declined, knowing that puppies were a pain to housebreak. They chewed shoes, furniture, and all the neighbors' newspapers. Our dachshund had recently been run over, and we were reluctant to become attached to another dog. The moment we laid eyes on the runt of the litter, however, we forgot about wall-to-wall newspapers and teeth marks on the woodwork. A mixture of poodle, Pomeranian, and an unidentified amorous canine fence climber, she had curly black hair, enormous, soulful, black eyes, and was not much bigger than my hand. She overwhelmed me with countless, puppy breath kisses, and proceeded to stake her claim on my husband's heart in the same endearing manner. She clamored over our three delighted sons and promptly christened the kitchen floor with a puddle twice her size.

Pepper was a fast learner, easily housebroken, and very affectionate. If there was a conflict in adapting to our household, it was between she and the cat. "Friday" had gotten used to growing up with our other animals, and they had all reached mid-life together, comfortable with one another and content to live and let live. Pepper teased, taunted, and tormented the lazy cat. She chased her, barked at her when she tried to nap, and generally made a pest of herself. Her need for a playmate was soon to be fulfilled, with the arrival of "Willie," a two year old dachshund in need of a home.

Willie and Pepper might have produced the world's most unusual puppies, but an unfortunate accident prevented that possibility. Pepper dashed into our neighbors' driveway one evening and was run over by the car. The distraught neighbor felt terrible and was surprised at my calm acceptance of the incident. At the time of the accident, we had undergone multiple family crises, and the poor dog's plight seemed minor. I explained our situation to our compassionate vet, and told him to do what he could for Pepper. She survived the night …

and although her pelvis was crushed and her left rear leg permanently lame, she raised her weary head at the sound of our voices and gave us reassuring kisses.

As the boys grew older, leaving home one by one, Pepper became more attached to my husband and me. She curled up by his feet every night when he read the paper, and jumped on my lap every time I sat down to watch television. I bought her some barrettes, and "she was pretty enough to win the dog show." Our shaggy, black haired little companion always ran on her three good legs to meet us when we drove into our driveway. She "talked" to us in a series of loud yelping and singing, telling us how much she missed us, and what had happened in the neighborhood while we were away. Terrified of storms, she always liked to be near us, for reassurance. If we were away, she would attempt to chew her way to safety. This resulted in many scoldings, and lots of door damage.

Recuperation from major surgery necessitated daily walking for my husband. The sight of a very large man, struggling to gain distance and strength, was even more poignant with a very small, crippled dog leashed to his hand. Pepper was his constant companion, keeping step with his ever increasing pace. She seemed to anticipate his vulnerability, and I'm certain they shared many confidences on their numerous walks. (I wonder if he suspected that she and I also had secret talks.)

Recently, a sudden, unexpected illness halted Pepper's kidney function, and as I held her on my lap for the last time, I thanked God for all the pleasure she brought to our family, and asked that He might consider having a very small puppy to walk close beside Him.

There once was a puppy named Pepper.

March 5, 1991

OLD DOGS AND NEW TRICKS

According to the people age conversion table, he is 75 years old. He is grey all around his face, and if we approach him from the right side, he can't see us until we're in front of him. When I call him in from the fenced-in back yard, he can no longer hear my voice, and I must search for him, and carry him up the same steps that he once raced several times each day. Willie, our aged dachshund, is entering his twilight years, and doesn't even qualify for Medicare.

He still thinks he can run, growl, bark, and explore with the best of the younger dogs. He visualizes himself, as most everyone does, still in his prime, and gets frustrated when his body won't cooperate with his wishes. Pain free, he leads a fairly comfortable existence, and still manages to give us a lot of pleasure and his unconditional devotion.

Due to his advanced years, and his limitations, we didn't want to leave him while we went out of town for a few days. Our oldest son has a dog pen for our grandpuppy, Dottie, and we agreed that Willie would be safe and well cared for if he stayed with them. I packed his prescription medication, along with a detailed list of how and when to administer it, his bowl, special old dog formula food, pillow, leash, and the vet's phone number. It was like sending a geriatric patient away to summer camp.

"Mom, don't worry about a thing, I'll take good care of Willie", our son said.

This uttered admonition, based on years of experience, gave me cause for immediate, constant worry.

Willie took one look at Dottie leaping like a kangaroo at the gate of the pen, and cast a disgruntled look at me through his good left eye. I wondered how I'd feel if someone decided to cage me up for a few days with one of my young, energetic nieces. Knowing what my reaction would have been, I marveled at the fact that Willie showed remarkable restraint and did not bite me on the leg. (Probably would have if he could have seen it.)

Things went along relatively well, until Dottie and her master decided to take Willie along for an evening stroll. Unfortunately, Dottie has yet to learn that she should walk with her human companion, rather than running back and forth between moving legs. She gallops along, straining at her leash, panting, and investigating every leaf, bug, and puddle along the way. Knowing that Willie was slow moving, and very docile, the unwise decision was made to let him mosey along without a leash. Less than two blocks from home, his attention distracted by Dottie's roadrunner antics, he noticed that Willie turned off to do some sightseeing in a short alley.

He incorrectly assumed that he would quickly return. After a few minutes, he called to him, and getting no response, began searching the alley, without success. How could an aged, arthritic, dog with three inch legs, move faster that a six foot, (consisting in most part of legs), physically fit man? The help of neighbors was enlisted, but after hours of fruitless hunting, the search was postponed.

Willie had embarked on a long journey through several blocks of back yards and quiet, unfamiliar territory, ending up on a very heavily traveled main thoroughfare. Concerned passersby were amazed when they noted the distance; they erroneously assumed he had traveled, from the home address on his metal bone shaped tag. After leaving several unanswered messages on our answering machine, they took Willie to the animal shelter for safekeeping.

After a sleepless night, and a trip to our house to check our phone messages, our very relieved son solved the mystery of the missing dachshund, and quickly reclaimed Willie from the shelter. Facing confinement once more with Dottie, I think Willie would have preferred taking his chances on the interstate.

Willie is home once more, and we just added a new medication to his daily doses. He and my husband now take the same prescription, except in different amounts. The druggist, trying to suppress his laughter, cautioned us not to confuse their dosages. If my husband starts to hike his leg while sniffing a tree, and Willie grabs the TV remote control and tunes in the weather channel, I'll know there's a mix up.

September 4, 1991

ACCIDENT PRONE PUP

*I*t was the end of the month, time to pay all those dreadful bills that were stuffed away. Opening the desk drawer, I am always depressed to find that they have not magically vanished, nor has any phantom benefactor marked them all "paid." They, like dirty dishes and dust, refuse to go away, and constantly accumulate in worrisome little piles in every household.

After writing the last of the checks, I heard the front door open, and knew that my husband was taking our aged Willie outside for his final doggie duty of the evening. Within seconds, I heard the sound of car brakes, barking dogs, and voices coming from the street. Before I could get the door opened completely, I was surprised to see our other dog, Hank, tearing past me into the kitchen. He stays in the fenced in back yard, and seldom goes near the front unless one of us is with him. His early desire to eat cars, as they passed him on the street, made him a poor risk for anything other than a fence or a sturdy leash.

As he ran past me, I saw a trail of blood and hurriedly followed him to find the source. His big hound eyes looked sadder than ever, as I gently petted him, and tried to locate an injured paw, or a nipped ear. As I tried to keep him calm, I was alarmed to see an increased amount of blood, and he certainly wasn't able to answer me, as I kept repeating my question, "Where are you hurt, feller?"

I snapped on the overhead kitchen light, and found the injury. His back legs, and stomach, had been severely skinned and cut. I couldn't leave him to get help from my husband, so I grabbed a towel, sat on the floor, and cradled the big injured animal's head in my lap, crying for him the tears I knew he wanted to shed. My shocked husband found us in a few minutes, as he came in with Willie. He had vainly attempted to stop Hank as he raced out the front door behind them, intent on catching a compact car turning in front of our house. The surprised driver stopped, apparently pinning Hank beneath the wheels of the car, but he managed to drag himself out, and retreat to the house, before anyone knew that he had been hit.

We tried to clean and bandage his wounds, but they were too severe and extensive. He needed a vet, but there were none to be had at this late evening hour, so we loaded him in the back, sheet-draped seat of the car, and drove him to the closest pet emergency clinic. He whimpered, shook, and attempted to administer self first aid to his wounds by licking them. How do you stop an animal from following his instinct, and convince him that he is doing more harm than good to himself?

Upon arrival at the clinic, we completed the admission form, told the attendant at the desk about Hank's poor judgment, and waited while the vet administered oxygen to a critically ill beagle puppy. While we waited in the treatment room, we coaxed Hank to stand on the animal scale, and were surprised to learn that our dog show reject weighed a hefty 71 pounds. It took both of us, the vet, and a strong attendant to hoist Hank onto the treatment table. His injuries were going to require anesthesia, surgery and an overnight stay at the clinic, and his aftercare would consist of antibiotics, frequent rebandaging, and a lot of supervision. Our plans to leave town in two days seemed to have acquired a sudden unexpected complication.

The estimated cost of putting our adventuresome pet back together was a shock. The next morning, we learned that the actual bill was more than it would have cost for another round trip plane ticket to New York. He had to have a follow up visit to his own vet, and was booked into the Fido Hilton for an infirmary suite while we were away.

We discussed Hank's misfortune, the unexpected extra expense of his treatment, and have decided to see if we can get him listed as a dependant on our income tax and group insurance ... at least until he's 18.

June 15, 1992

DOG HEAVEN BOUND

*I*t has been said that true happiness begins after the kids leave home and the dog dies. Our kids have left, and the dog just died, and I'm finding it difficult, for more reasons than the most obvious, to turn cartwheels.

The children have left, one by one, to make their own lives, which is the natural course of things. The house has become quieter, and there are dry bath towels and shampoo back in the bathroom. There are no stereo speakers rattling the windows, and clean drinking glasses are in the kitchen cabinet instead of piled up, dirty, in the sink. The only time the telephone rings, it's either a computer questionnaire or a rug shampoo offer, and the refrigerator door stays shut for hours. The pizza delivery man has to ask directions to our house on the rare occasions we order in, rather than putting the car on auto pilot, and we now have grass growing over the bare patches in the yard where cars used to be parked for amateur repairs.

The natural companion for boys is a dog. We had three boys, hence we had three dogs. Willie, our dachshund, was a foundling who came to us when he was about 2 years old, and the boys were in their pre, early and late teen years. Had the poor dog realized what he was coming into, he probably would have taken his chances on remaining homeless. He thrived on pizza crust, peanut butter, bologna, and table scraps, (when there were any), and managed to sneak into the boys' rooms and find a warm spot in one of their beds. It was rather difficult to believe the excuse of "he jumped in the bed while I was sleeping," because we thought his short stumpy legs made it impossible to propel himself to the top half of a bunk bed. I re-evaluated his capabilities, however, after he managed to leap the distance between the kitchen butcher block and the floor and feast on an entire pound of Muenster cheese set out for dinner guests.

He chased his own tail, bicycles, skateboards, and raced after the boys every time they were in the yard. He loved to roll up, cocoon style, in bedding;

if his own were not handy, he would pull the bedspread or blanket from an unsuspecting, sleeping family member. His favorite spot, on cold nights was in front of the fireplace or kerosene heater. He'd slumber peacefully while his short reddish brown hair baked from the heat. The cat, who didn't much care for him when he arrived, soon accepted him, and they occasionally shared dinner from the same bowl.

He wasn't much of a watchdog, because he barked at anything that moved, including the other two family dogs. Their domain consisted mainly of our fenced in back yard, which he fearlessly protected from birds, rabbits, chipmunks, and butterflies. The only time he ever ventured away from our street, he was apprehended by the pound patrol, and had to be bailed out.

As he grew older, and there was less activity in the house and backyard, he enjoyed several daily snoozes in the sunshine. When rain or chilly weather prevented him from being out in the elements, he would seek the shelter and protection of our storage barn. He had a wool blanket, and would wrap himself snugly in it until we arrived home from work to bring him inside to the warmth and comfort of the kitchen. His red coat began to show more flecks of grey, and he began to cough more.

The vet took x-rays and when she brought them into the treatment room, and put them up to the light, we sensed a problem.

"Willie has an enlarged heart, and his lungs are collecting fluid, that's why he coughs a lot".

We administered his prescriptions each morning, (along with a half an aspirin for his arthritis) hidden inside bite size pieces of hot dog. For two years he managed to function reasonably well, with the medication, and our help with the steps.

Then we noticed he was having difficulty with his vision and hearing. He quickly lost all of his sight, and most of his hearing, and we knew what had to be done to spare him of additional incapacities. We postponed his final visit to the vet's office, and made the car trip with heavy hearts.

We stood with him as he too quickly eased into a peaceful, permanent sleep and used up all the available tissues as we told our faithful little companion farewell. I think dogs must have a special spot in heaven for the devotion they give in return for a little bit of love ... I hope so.

July 5, 2013

Birds Of A Feather

I erroneously believed that an ornithologist was a doctor who diagnosed and treated certain parts of the human body, but only recently did I learn that the term refers to a person who scientifically studies birds. The dictionary advises that they differ from birdwatchers because they collect more in-depth data. Bird watching is a fascinating hobby that I would love to learn, but haven't yet studied. I can readily spot and correctly identify a redbird, bluebird, robin, hummingbird, seagull, parrot, woodpecker, or a crow, but beyond those easily recognizable species, I cannot differentiate between a wren and a barn swallow.

I lost interest in birds after our pet parakeet died many years ago, but it renewed again after a mourning dove decided to take up her annual nesting on our patio. It was such a joy to watch her and her mate guarding the eggs, feeding the newly hatched baby, and then seeing the fledgling discover that he could actually fly on his own. She was a repeat visitor for several years, and we always looked forward to her presence, until last summer when I found the remnants of her nest, broken egg shell and feathers on the ground. Apparently a predator bird, likely a hawk, attacked her, and if she survived, she moved to safer surroundings, which both infuriated and saddened me. I kept a sharp watch out for the mean bird who had so viciously confronted this sweet and gentle creature, but never was able to show him my wrath. If he ever shows his face again, he will have to deal with me and a sturdy tennis racket.

My neighbor recently came over to tell me some exciting news. "I saw an eagle this morning when my sister and I were fishing down near your dock." Not only had she seen it, but she had done a video that she posted on the internet. She showed me pictures on her phone, and I was very impressed with what I saw. She told me he was a young eagle and had not yet gotten his white neck feathers, so to be on the lookout for him again. Little did she know that the only eagle I had ever seen was the logos on postage stamps, a commuter airplane, and a dollar bill. I wasn't sure how large it was, or what I might look for to recognize this symbol of our nation, but I wasn't going to let that deter me in my efforts.

Bright and early the following morning, I made my usual cup of tea, put on my bathrobe and positioned myself where I had a good view of our back yard. Sure enough, I was astonished to see a huge dark bird land atop our dock, just as she had said he might. Without a camera handy, I resorted to my old cell phone, which leaves a lot to be desired with its photo taking capabilities. (It is a phone, after all, which explains why it doesn't do what a camera should.) I was reluctant to move any closer for fear that I might scare the eagle away, so I just started snapping pictures from my vantage point. Within a few minutes of my sighting, another eagle appeared beside the first one. This was certainly my lucky day, I thought, as I tried not to hyperventilate. Rather quickly, more of the birds gathered in the same spot. Now I don't know much about birds, as I have previously stated, but I had never heard of a flock of eagles, so I quickly dashed inside to grab some binoculars for a closer look, resisting the impulse to awaken and alert the entire neighborhood to my good fortune.

By the time I got back outside, the "flock of eagles" had descended to the ground and were congregating in one area. Through my binoculars, I was able to see that they were feasting on some dead fish near the edge of the water. It was then, to my disgust and horror, I realized that the birds I had mistaken for eagles were actually turkey buzzards. I immediately deleted the pictures from my phone and decided that I needed to go to the library and check out a book on birdwatching.

August 29, 2011

Holey Moley

Walking across our front lawn, I noticed some rather suspicious looking holes that had appeared. There were also a few areas of raised dirt that were very soft when I stepped on them. Flashback to childhood and time spent with my grandfather in his fruit orchard when I had seen similar evidence of underground critters making themselves at home beneath the surface of the earth. I knew without a doubt that we had moles infiltrating our yard.

Although they are very illusive little mammals, I had witnessed my grandfather and his pet collie, Leo, flushing the small blind moles from beneath the ground out into the open and carting them off in a wheelbarrow into the woods that surrounded the orchard and house, or killing them with a garden hoe, which I hated to see. Not having a four legged canine pet to assist me in my hunt for moles, I kept a vigilant eye out for sightings of the tiny creatures that were wrecking havoc all across the grassy lawn. I recalled seeing their soft, brown, shiny fur and how it didn't seem to match their unattractive faces and flesh colored webbed paws that eerily resembled unmanicured human hands.

Returning from the mail box one afternoon, I caught a glimpse of something moving in the grass. Closer observation revealed what I had hoped it would: a busy mole was attempting to dig a new entrance to one of the existing tunnels. Perhaps he was a visiting relative from out of town who wanted to surprise his family, but without thinking twice and feeling no fear, I reached down and grabbed him by his tail. Assuming incorrectly that because they were sightless they wouldn't bite, I very quickly learned that their survival instinct kicks in when threatened, and his little head swung around quickly and he chomped down on my finger. I don't think they have upper teeth, but he did a pretty good job with his lower incisors, and I certainly wasn't going to verify the number and position of his teeth at that moment.

Naturally, I dropped him immediately, ran for the house where I washed the bite thoroughly with soap and water, applied antibiotic ointment and a bandage. It wasn't a deep wound, but knowing that his primary diet consisted of earthworms, grubs and other yucky insects, and that he most certainly had a lot of dirt in his mouth, I put in a call for my physician. After I made him promise not to laugh when I told him what I had done, he took a deep breath and we agreed it might be wise for me to take a round of antibiotics which he would phone in to our pharmacy so I could get started on them. Since it was the weekend, and I had no recollection, I was to call the office on Monday and ask when I had my last tetanus shot. On Monday, I rolled up my sleeve, gritted my teeth and received my necessary vaccine. By Tuesday, I had forgotten about the mole bite and focused on the goose egg sized knot that resulted from the shot. The mole was having the last laugh on me, it seemed.

Determined more than ever to evict our unwelcome tenants from the yard, I have learned that there are all sorts of ideas on how to get rid of moles. Cat litter, human hair, bleach, fruit flavored sticks of chewing gum, moth balls, vibrating pinwheels stuck into the ground, pickle juice, and a mixture of castor oil, dish soap and cayenne pepper are a few of the ones I will try individually and collectively. Short of getting an owl, a cat, or Indiana Jones to help me hunt them down, I fervently hope that one or more of the home remedies do the trick.

The mole group is currently still active in our yard, likely plotting how to outsmart me, but I read that they do not have this problem in Ireland, so I think I shall research the legend of how St. Patrick drove all the snakes out of the country, assuming they took the moles along with them. Then I'll visit the nearest home and garden center and seek out an effective and humane way to banish them forever from my lawn and my life.

RETURN OF THE DOVES

ive years ago, during Holy Week, following the sudden and unexpected death of our nephew, I wrote about the dove that suddenly appeared and set up housekeeping on our patio. For us, it was a tangible sign of the presence of the Holy Spirit bringing us consolation and comfort. We erroneously thought then that doves had a short life span, and that once "Cooey" left the confines of our place, we would never see her again, so we took delight in watching her each day, and snapped numerous photos of her and her offspring.

We are surprised and happy to report that she not only returned the following year to hatch another set of twins, but has been a repeat tenant each and every spring, relocating from the wicker shelf amidst ceramic frogs to establishing a new home in a terra cotta wall mounted flower pot beneath our carport. Safely nestled among the artificial flowers I arranged, she is hidden from the view of passersby and the elements don't affect her, as she is protected from rain, wind and even the hot sun. She has grown accustomed to our greetings to her each time we arrive or depart, and has even allowed my husband to pet her on occasion. She is still a bit jumpy around the curious grandchildren, as are we occasionally, but she does allow them to be lifted up to peer into her nest.

At first, we thought she was not the same bird, but her distinct markings convinced us otherwise. We believed each newcomer to be one of the previous year's offspring returning to their birthplace, much like the swallows that return to Capistrano. However, since that year of her first appearance, we have learned that mourning doves can live between seven and 11 years, and there is one recorded notation of one that lived for 31 plus years. They are also monogamous, mating for life. We awaken to the long recitation of cooing that her husband, whom I dubbed "Mr. Gray," tirelessly calls out to attract her attention, and it isn't long before we see them taking turns sitting on their eggs in their permanent home. He, during the day, and she, like most mothers, takes the nightshift.

All other years, once the baby hatches, becomes a fledgling in about two weeks, and leaves the nest, they disappear until the following spring. Not so this year. As of this writing, "Cooey" has just hatched her third baby for 2010. She no sooner vacates her space before we hear his low, mournful calls and they are back again. After doing a bit of research on our rather prolific couple, we have found out that a pair of doves can produce up to six broods per year. Our little happily mated set seem to be going for the world's record this year.

Doves are a symbol of peace and tranquility, and I believe that our doves come to us when we need assurance of God's love and care for us and those we love. It was a revelation for me to see the symbolism, especially in the aftermath of the recent flood, in the biblical reference to Noah's dispatch of a dove, as directed by God after the Great Flood:

"Then he sent forth a dove from him, to see if the waters had subsided from the face of the ground; but the dove found no place to set her foot, and she returned to him to the ark, for the waters were still on the face of the whole earth. So he put forth his hand and took her and brought her into the ark with him. He waited another seven days, and again he sent forth the dove out of the ark; and the dove came back to him in the evening, and lo, in her mouth a freshly plucked olive leaf; so Noah knew that the waters had subsided from the earth. Then he waited another seven days, and sent forth the dove; and she did not return to him anymore." (Genesis 8:8-12)

THREE LITTLE FISHIES

*W*e recently had the pleasure of keeping our three grandsons while their parents were out of town for a few days. The boys, all still in elementary school, brought all of their trappings with them: clothes, uniforms, sports equipment, toothbrushes, stuffed animals, toys, and the ever present electronic games. In addition to their necessities and diversions, they also brought along their most recent pets — three goldfish, each one in its own individual glass bowl. When their grandfather suggested that the fish might enjoy the company of one another, and all move into a communal bowl, that idea was quickly vetoed by a three to one vote. The boys explained that they each like to take their own fish to their respective rooms at home and the fish liked their private spaces. The fact that they would all be bunking in together while staying at our place seemed irrelevant. (We were unsure how the fish felt about this, but went with the majority vote.)

The water receptacles and their residents were lined up next to each other on the kitchen counter, near the fluorescent light to give them the effect of sunshine. I was careful not to place the bowls too close to the light, fearing the water temperature might get too warm. We had an aquarium many years ago for our sons, and could not understand why we kept having such a high birth rate among the black mollies. Turned out the temperature of the water was too high and it caused them to multiply like rabbits. Since our "grandfish" were each living alone, this wouldn't be a cause for concern, but I'm pretty sure fish can't sweat, so I didn't want to take a chance on them getting overheated.

Fish are great pets. They don't make noise, don't have to be housebroken, can't jump on the furniture, don't have to be neutered or declawed, and they don't chew on shoes. The amount of food and living space they require is miniscule, no annual shots are required, and they don't have to be walked when it's rainy and cold outside. On the down side, however, it's difficult to interact with a fish. They can't fetch, keep your feet warm on a cold night, or learn pet tricks.

There are no costumes for fish to wear for Halloween, and they don't greet their owners with adoring eyes or wagging tails.

Everything seemed to be going smoothly with our finny little houseguests, until the second day of their visit when I was summoned into the kitchen to examine a very dormant goldfish. He didn't move. His gills were not moving, and his tail was absolutely still. His master was summoned, and we decided that "Phil Jr." might just be sleeping. We would check on him again in about 15 minutes, as I estimated that would be the appropriate period of time for a "fish nap".

Time passed, and still no signs of movement or life from the fish. Unlike previously expired fish, Phil Jr. wasn't floating belly up on the surface of the water, and I was unsure of where the pulse of a fish might be, so it was hard to determine if he had actually passed away. Not wanting to take any chances, we opted to wait until after dinner to see how he looked.

The unanimous decision was that Phil Jr. had met with the same tragic fate as his deceased predecessor, Phil Sr. I was advised that fish flushing was no longer environmentally or ecologically an acceptable method of disposing of the dearly departed, so I offered the options of placing the remains in an ear-ring box and interring him in my patio tomato pot, or cremating him in the chiminea. Neither of these options appealed to my bereft grandson, and he opted for cryogenics until the rest of the immediate family returned home. He wanted them to assemble for a private burial in their family "plot" on the hill behind their house.

Phil Jr. was lovingly placed in a small zipper freezer bag and carefully deposited in our utility room freezer right between the lima beans and the popsicles, but thoughtfully distanced from the frozen fish sticks. His bowl was cleaned and wrapped in newspaper until a suitable replacement could be acquired. I had to break the sad news of his untimely demise to my son and his wife and explained that the body was on ice until they returned to claim it.

We don't know if the graveside services for Phil Jr. have taken place yet, but we extend our sympathy to our grandson, who is still mourning the loss of his beloved pet. I offer him the sage advice of Forrest Gump, who said "My Mama always said you've got to put the past behind you before you can move on."

April 27, 1986

SOFT SPOT FOR WEBBED FEET

*M*y better judgment told me to not do it; my maternal instincts seconded the motion. There I was, tricked into looking at baby ducks in the pet shop window, vainly attempting to pry two small noses and four little hands from the glass.

"We promise, we promise, Mom, to take care of these ducks, if you'll only let us have them."

Although our pervious experience with Easter ducks and bunnies had not been too successful, the solemn pleas of my children, and the appeal of those fuzzy, yellow ducklings weakened my defenses. We purchased the ducks and necessary food, and had a lengthy discussion en route to the house about the responsibility of pet ownership. I felt confident that I would not eventually qualify for the duck mascot at the Peabody Hotel.

After settling the ducks in their shoe box dwelling, the boys decided they needed names. "Timmy" and "Saskanita" were the chosen names. Although we never did understand where they came up with the latter, we knew that no other duck would have the same name. The newspapers were changed frequently that first day, due to the ducks tipping over their jar lid watering trough numerous times. A night light was plugged in over their box, for warmth, and we fell asleep hearing the chirping sounds of the two baby birds that now resided in our bathroom.

As summer arrived, the ducks had progressed from their first small box, through several larger ones, and had taken up residence in a makeshift cage beneath an old playpen turned upside down. They thrived on dry cereal, crackers and an occasional peanut butter and jelly sandwich.

In addition to caring for two former duck lovers and a small baby, I had fallen heir to the large, quacking creatures who dominated our backyard. They took over the wading pool and chased the dog and cat. The idea of a duck dinner became more appealing as the hot summer days drug on.

Timmy flew over the back fence one afternoon and landed in the front yard. He waddled over to investigate the neighbor's large, lazy dog, and met with an unpleasant demise. We buried him in the back yard, amidst the remains of several, smaller predecessors of assorted animals, and prayed he would go to "duck heaven".

Saskanita grew lonely and depressed. (It is extremely difficult to judge the emotions of a duck, but the diagnosis seemed to satisfy the children.)

"Boys, we think Saskanita would be happier living with some other ducks, so Dad and I will take him/her to a place where he will be with friends."

We set Saskanita down on the riverbank and he/she quickly glided into the water, paddled over to the other web-footed inhabitants, flapped his wings loudly and gave us a contented farewell "quack". At least he had been spared the fate of winding up at a pillow factory. Our consciences were at rest.

The pet shop was permanently off limits, lest I succumb to further temptation. I had not anticipated the box of puppies in front of the grocery store, however ... .

I cannot see them, but I know they are there,
Those angels and saints who are everywhere.
They hold my hand and hear my pleas,
Whether I'm in my chair or on my knees.
They take my requests and stand before the Throne
Asking Jesus to help me, so I'm not alone.
Whenever I have fear or am filled with doubt,
They're always on call to help me out.

—Copyright © 2014 Mary Margaret Lambert

Make friends with the angels,
who though invisible are always with you.
Often invoke them, constantly praise them,
and make good use of their help and assistance
in all your temporal and spiritual affairs.

—Saint Francis de Sales, Patron Saint of writers and artists

ANGELS AND SAINTS

Chapter

LOOKING FOR ST. ANTHONY

"Tony, Tony, look around, something's lost, and can't be found." This little prayer/poem, memorized in my early childhood years, seems to be my daily recitation. St. Anthony, known by many as the patron saint of lost items, must surely wince when he hears my voice reaching heavenward in petition.

My evasive possessions range from small items, such as the car keys, to the ultimate loss, the car itself. Whenever I go to a shopping center, or any large parking area, I always experience sheer panic as I search the endless aisles of shiny autos in an effort to recognize my own. I got so excited on one of my frequent grocery trips at finding the car right away, I drove all the way home before I realized I'd forgotten to go to the "pick-up" area to claim my parcels.

I recall a day that my elderly grandmother and great aunt visited a local theme park. Upon leaving the park, they had no recollection of where they had parked the car, so they flagged down the horse mounted patrolman in the parking lot. He asked, "What is the make and color of your automobile, and do you know the license tag number?" They naively responded, "It's blue, has four doors, some dents, and a towel across the front seat." I figure if he found it from that description, I'd certainly like to see him on duty in my grocery parking lot.

At our house, whenever an item is "misplaced," no matter who the owner is, it is assumed that I should always know its new location. "Mom, where's my plaid shirt?" "Who moved my tackle box?" "Have you seen my razor?" "What happened to the dog's leash?"

As I rarely have inclination to shave, put on a plaid flannel shirt, and take the dog fishing, I find this strangely amusing. Now, granted, St. Anthony and I have a wonderful friendship going, but even he, with all his saintly abilities, must find it difficult to find all the things we lose.

St. Anthony not only is instrumental in helping to find lost articles, but this beloved disciple of St. Francis of Assisi answers countless prayers for the return of lost hope, faith, and love. He seems, to me, to be a wonderful "all purpose" saint for almost any intention one might have. A portion of a prayer to him states, "O blessed St. Anthony, the grace of God had made you a powerful advocate in all our needs, and the patron of the restoring of things lost or stolen. I turn to you today with childlike love and deep confidence. You are the counselor of the erring, the comforter of the troubled, the healer of the sick, the refuge of the fallen. Help me in my present need. I recommend what I have lost to your care, in the hope that God will restore it to me if it is his holy will."

Since I have difficulty finding my prayer book at times, I most often resort to "Tony, Tony, look around," and he must surely hear me because he never fails to answer.

January 25, 1987

SAINT OF EXPECTANT MOTHERS AND BABIES

*A*s with most first time parents-to-be, my husband and I were thrilled at the prospect of having a baby of our very own. Although we were young and living on a shoestring, we were confident that our baby would be the most beautiful, wonderful infant in the entire world. I felt fantastic, and despite words of caution from my gentle, understanding obstetrician, we set out on a summer vacation to New York to visit some of my husband's relatives. We loaded our 1955 Nash station wagon, hoping it would survive the additional mileage on its already filled odometer, and set out on our fateful journey.

We reached our destination, stopping overnight once, in two days driving time. Exhausted, we chatted briefly with our host and hostess, and retired for a much needed night of rest. I was awakened by an uncomfortable damp feeling beneath me, and I sat up in the bed. I was horrified to discover that I was hemorrhaging, and in grave danger of losing our baby. After several vain attempts at reaching a physician who would come to minister to my needs, my husband and his cousins carried me down the long narrow stairs, and tenderly laid me in the back of their station wagon. On the long, seemingly endless drive to the hospital, I recited the rosary non-stop.

The rules of the hospital prevented my husband, or any family member, from being with me in the labor room. I was terrified, but feeling the movements of my baby within my rotund abdomen reassured me that he was safe and not ready to leave me yet. The nurse prepared me for delivery, although I was not in labor, and once more, I used my trembling, cold fingers as counters for the Hail Mary's of my calming rosary. Then I was finally moved to a regular room, I clung to my young, equally frightened husband, and drew newfound strength from his very presence beside me.

After four days, I was dismissed with the strict admonition from the maternity medical staff to remain in bed for the remaining three and a half months of my pregnancy. Refusing offers from concerned parents to fly us home, we purchased an air mattress, made a bed for me in the cargo area of our small, temperamental station wagon, and headed home. Less than fifty miles into our journey, the mattress came apart at the seams, and we made a makeshift "nest" where I rode for the remaining 850 miles.

My doctor concurred with the earlier prognosis, so I went to my parents' home, where, in a rented hospital bed, I would wait for my baby to grow to term. After three more trips to the hospital for complications, my great aunt, a Dominican nun, brought me two medals: one of St. Anne, mother of the Blessed Virgin, and the other of St. Gerard Majella, the patron of motherhood. Through the prayerful intercession of this newfound saint, along with that of my beloved St. Francis, our tiny son was delivered safely, and lived long enough to be baptized. After his death, and a subsequent miscarriage, it was doubtful that I would ever conceive, or carry to term, another child.

Our three "miracle" babies are grown now, but I continue to ask St. Gerard for assistance in the trials of parenthood. My story is not an unusual one. It has been experienced, with varying pertinent personal facts, by countless numbers of faithful St. Gerard advocates. I have lost count of the number of medals and pamphlets I have passed along to others in need of his help, but I am always delighted to hear news of another St. Gerard success story. After I gave a medal and prayer leaflet to one particular friend who was experiencing difficulties in her pregnancy, not only did she deliver her firstborn son safely, but returned the medal after she had two more children in rapid succession.

Whenever I see the name of Gerard listed on any school program, I know that the parents of that young person have also experienced the wonderful intercession of my miraculous saint.

June 18, 1990

ANGEL OF GOD

"*A*ngel of God, my guardian dear, to whom His love commits me here, ever this day be at my side, to light and guard, to rule and guide. Amen"

It was a simple little childish prayer, and the dear nuns saw to it that we said it each and every afternoon just before we marched out the doors of the elementary classrooms. After moving onto bigger and better things in life, such as high school, the reality of an ever present guardian angel hanging out with us just didn't seem too appealing, so the little prayer was committed to memory and abandoned.

After comparing the spiritual messages conveyed in "It's A Wonderful Life" versus that of "The Exorcist," I decided that it might be wise to get on more familiar terms, and I became re-acquainted with my faithful guardian angel. She was more than willing to talk with me, and I soon came to know a great deal about her. I'm certain that on the day my soul was united with my body, she begged and pleaded for an easier guardianship.

"Please, Gabriel can't you and Michael give me an easy soul to take care of? I'd really do well with someone like Joan of Arc, Mother Theresa (her angel says she's a dream to work with), Carrie Nation, or even Bess Truman. I need to gain some points here in heaven, and trade in my old robe, crooked halo, and broken harp. I can't even earn my wings until one of my humans follows all the rules."

Her answer, in the year 1940, was evident as she hovered above the plump baby girl with the thick cap of straight black hair. She looked down on the swollen, red face of her newest assignment, and heard the doctor wonder aloud how he managed to save both the mother and the child in this difficult delivery. The angel smiled. Maybe this wouldn't be so bad, after all.

It is said that angels have no sense of humor. This has to be incorrect, especially in the case of my angel. I think my angel must be a bit different from all the other host of heavenly creatures, or else she would surely have a better job. There must be angels who look like the cherubs on Valentine cards and still others who are powerfully built, with great massive wings, and beautiful voices. I think mine must look a lot like a Cabbage Patch doll. She probably has grey hair, due to years of frustration, a faded robe in need of mending, and her halo leans permanently on a tilted angle. At heavenly host choir practice, she must be assigned to the lighting crew, as her voice is raspy from years of yelling into an ear that turns deaf on her most of the time.

When the other angels get together to discuss their frustrating assignments, I think my angel must snicker at their complaints and secretly wish for their problems. She is most likely the last to make her weekly reports, and I hope she cheats a bit, (in my favor, of course), when she lists the shortcomings and faults of her earthly creature.

Her feet are probably sore from all the walking she must do to keep pace with me, and the only time she gets to enjoy the luxury of flying, (because she still remains wingless), I talk to her constantly on the airplane and make all kinds of deals with her to get me back safely. She always encourages me to ask for a window seat to allow her to gaze out at the clouds and wave at her friends, but, as usual, I override her suggestion, and avoid any reminders of the distance between me and the ground.

We've come a long way together, this tired old angel and me. I listen to her more often than I used to, but I still tend to defy her suggestions, make a mess of things, and then relentlessly implore her to bail me out again. I doubt if she'll ever get her wings on this job, but she certainly must have earned a few extra stars in her halo, and perhaps if St. Peter takes a fishing trip, she'll sneak me in a side window near the Pearly Gates.

July 6, 1993

WHY ST. PETER HOLDS THE KEYS
TO HEAVEN INSTEAD OF ME

Baby's favorite first rattle is often the item that will give him the most cause for stress in later life. The jingling sound made by a set of keys, hastily pulled from Mom's purse or Dad's pocket, will soothe a fussy little one quicker than any other toy. Only later in life does one long to hear that familiar, and all too often, evasive noise when frantically searching for a lost key ring.

Houses, apartments, cars, trunks, boats, offices, briefcases, luggage, jail cells, files, freezers, and computers all require keys to open them, and a responsible owner to keep up with them. The most maddening experience in the world is to be 10 minutes late for an appointment and unable to find the keys. Sure, you know just where you put them, but some mysterious little gremlins must have moved them. Of course there's always the extra set, but they seem to have also vanished. I am indebted to St. Anthony for all eternity, and he knows when he hears my voice to enlist his helpers in the search for misplaced keys.

The first day of school for our oldest son was a major milestone for the entire family. We all got up very early, ate a big breakfast, carefully packed a well balanced lunch in the shiny, yellow school bus lunch box; put all the new unmarked books, primary tablet, and fat pencils in the new book satchel. I cried as I watched him and his Dad pull out of the driveway, and bemoaned the fact that this day marked the beginning of his growing up. The morning quickly passed as I did laundry, washed dishes, and tended to the needs of my 4-year-old and his baby brother. Still in my gown and robe, I dashed out to pick up the morning paper. I heard the front door slam and lock as I started back up the steps.

I rang the doorbell, and heard the devilish giggle from the other side of the locked door.

"Let Mommy in, honey. Turn the door handle so I can get back in the

41

house", I implored, trying very hard not to let the anger and fear I felt create more tears.

Silence from the living room convinced me to try the garage doors. I knew they were locked, but I was hoping against all hope that I could pull hard enough to disengage the locking mechanism and get in the house through the basement. No luck. I ran around to the front windows and looked inside to see if the baby was still safe in his crib, and his big brother was still near the door.

It was nearly time to pick up the first grader from his first half day of school. I, in my leopard velour robe, with uncombed hair, and unwashed face, dashed over to my single, childless neighbor's house, and assaulted her with a deluge of breathless "first day school, locked out, kids in house, need ladder, come quick", before I ran back to our front porch. Certain that I had finally experienced some sort of breakdown, she called another neighbor, and they arrived with a ladder. I gave her directions to the school, and persuaded her to pick up the first grader while I balanced myself atop the ladder. My other neighbor stayed to steady me as I climbed through an unlocked kitchen window, and assured me that we'd laugh about this in years to come.

The 4-year-old thought the entire episode was great fun, and the baby was playing happily in his crib, blissfully unaware of the severe stress his mother was experiencing. At the urging of my neighbors, I had extra keys made for each of them, and another one to "hide" for emergencies. (Somebody always managed to use the extra one, and lose it, so I was a familiar customer at the hardware store.) The neighbors also suggested if I was going to be running up and down the street before I dressed, I might consider buying myself a better looking robe, and stash a comb in the pocket.

I have managed to throw my car keys down a garbage chute while dumping trash for a relative, lock my keys in the car, and lose all the keys to my luggage. We have crawled in storm windows, and squeezed through narrow door openings; spent hours fishing for a car door lock with a bent coat hanger and sifted through garbage in search of keys. The locksmith and I are on a first name basis. In one drawer, we have dozens of keys, but no idea of what they unlock, so we keep them "just in case."

With my luck, if I ever make it to the pearly gates of heaven, they will be locked, and St. Peter will be out searching for his lost keys. I do hope they have a window and a ladder handy ... just in case. I'll try to wear my best looking robe.

42

March 31, 1993

MARY, THE IDEAL MOTHER

Holy week, the culmination of Lent and the reflective time when we call to mind the suffering and death of Jesus. If our Lenten sacrifices haven't been too impressive, and we've faltered in our fasting and prayer life, we can make amends during this solemn time preceding glorious Easter. We all remember how Jesus suffered in the Garden at Gethsemeni, how he was tortured, betrayed, humiliated, mocked, scourged, and ultimately put to death. While these unspeakable actions were being directed at her son, how did Mary cope with the unrelenting pain?

I won't enter into the controversial debate concerning the virginity of Mary. I'll leave that to the more learned theologians and biblical scholars who have researched it extensively. I'm quite content to know merely that Mary was the mother of Jesus, period. She was a teenaged Jewish maiden, chosen by God to be the earthly mother for His son. Together with Joseph, they would be the caregivers, providers, teachers, guardians, human role models, and parents for Jesus. Most likely she didn't realize that she would be the inspiration for every Mother that followed her.

When they were called, from Galilee, to go to Bethlehem for the census, and there was no other place for her to give birth to her child, she slept in a stable and made him a bed on the hay. After escaping Herod's murderous wrath by fleeing into Egypt, they lived in Nazareth. There, the daily routine of wife, mother, and homemaker evolved, as Mary bathed, fed, and clothed her son. I suppose they would call it "bonding" now. As her little boy learned to crawl, and then to walk, she probably held his tiny hand in her own, and guided his every faltering step. When he fell, and bumped his head, she was there to soothe the hurt and tend to all the other inevitable scraped knees and bruises of childhood.

If the weather allowed, perhaps Mary packed a picnic lunch for she, Joseph and Jesus to enjoy. They may have spent time lying in the warm sun, sharing food she had prepared for the three of them, and watched their young son learn to climb a tree, or skip a stone across the river. As Mary watched attentively, Joseph may have shown the boy how to catch a fish for dinner. He taught Jesus the carpentry skill that was their livelihood.

When they lost him in the Temple in Jerusalem during Passover, Mary surely spent many anxious hours until they located him speaking to the elders. In a crowd, there were many places for a twelve year old boy to disappear, and certainly Mary imagined her son in all of the worst ones. When they finally found him, did she react as any other mother by tearfully embracing him, and then admonishing him with, "don't you ever wander off from us like that again, young man." Did the other children badger and tease Jesus? Being a normal child, I'm sure he endured his share of cruelty and peer pressure. When he came home in tears because he wasn't invited to a birthday celebration, or asked to join in a neighborhood game, Mary was there to console him.

As Jesus grew into manhood, Mary watched him preach and perform miracles, and she knew that her job as his guardian was completed. While he prayed in the Garden of Gethsemane, the young, widowed Mary must have been at home, waiting, worrying, and praying for her son to have the strength to endure his suffering. As the crown of thorns was placed upon his head and blood streamed into his saddened eyes, she must have felt every thorn pierce her own aching heart. When he carried his cross to Calvary, falling under its weight many times, she could only watch his struggle and be consoled by friends who remained by her side. She would have willingly died herself carrying it for him, if she could.

While her 33-year-old son hung, crucified before her, she knelt at the foot of the cross, powerless to save him from his tortured death. This Son of God was her son also, but her maternal love for him yielded to the will of the Father. When she held his broken, limp body in her arms for the final time, before they took him from her, how she must have mourned. Three days later, with her friends and those of Jesus, Mary went to the tomb. Imagine her surprise and joy when the angel told them,

"Do not be frightened. I know you are looking for Jesus the crucified, but he is not here. He has been raised, exactly as he promised. Come and see the place where he was laid. Then go quickly and tell his disciples: 'He has been raised from the dead and now goes before you to Galilee, where you will see him.' That is the message I have for you."

The Resurrection of Jesus was also the consolation of his mother.

MERCIFUL HEAVENS

*A*ngel First Class Timothy was in a quandary. He had just recently been promoted from Assistant Angel In Charge Of Rain to head of the department, and ever since his first day in the new position, there had been a sharp decline in rain orders from the head office. From the United States of America, in particular, there were countless pleas coming in daily to use his influence to end their drought, but until he got the order, he couldn't release one single drop of rain.

He watched billions of dollars worth of farming land dry up, and the farmers sell dairy cattle because they couldn't afford to buy the hay to feed them. He saw barges stranded in shrinking waters of once mighty rivers, and he looked on, helplessly, as forests became as brittle as matchsticks, ready to ignite from one fiery spark into a raging inferno. He knew in his heart that there was only one thing for him to do; he must go to the Lord and ask Him to help ease this situation.

With trembling wings, Timothy took a seat before the Lord and began to state his reason for being in His presence. He realized that this could mean a demotion for him, but he summoned every bit of his supernatural courage, and blurted out his concerns.

"Lord, I know you're awfully busy, and I wouldn't trouble you for anything except an emergency," he said respectfully.

"There are a lot of your people in some serious trouble and they have need of your immediate help, sir. These people are not as accustomed to famine and drought as some of the others, and I think we need to examine their plight."

The Lord listened patiently as Timothy continued.

"These Americans are very smart people, Lord. They have lots of scientists, and all kinds of sophisticated equipment to predict the weather. They all have some sort of electronic picture machine that they watch, and it displays the image and voice of a person telling them what the temperature is and what they can expect all week long from the weather. It shows pictures of clouds, and, in the winter, there is a strange looking little bird that talks about the schools that are closed because of snow."

Timothy watched as the Lord's eyes looked at hin, and he lost his sense of fear as he talked on.

"I know they think they are self-reliant, Lord, and they seem to forget how dependent they are upon you. They have invented artificial everything, from body organs to sugar. They have created flowers and plants from man-made fibers to duplicate your own live versions, and they have even tampered with the process of procreation. They have invented cordless appliances, powerful motor cars, great winged crafts that transport them all around the world and into space, and even machines that can do all of their office work automatically. They can cook their meals in a few seconds in a special cooker, and they use a plastic card to replace their currency. They can do anything, Lord, but they cannot make it rain … please help them."

The Lord looked at Timothy, and He thought about all the things that he had told Him about these citizens of a most blessed country. He realized that these Americans were spoiled, and they took His goodness for granted far too often. He thought about their goodness, and their evils, their weaknesses, and their strengths … and most of all He thought about how much He loved them, and His eyes filled with tears and spilled down into the barren rivers and the parched farmland.

Timothy summoned a special angel detail work crew, in response to the Lord's wishes. He suggested to Timothy that perhaps these distressed mortals needed yet another reminder of the responsibility they had to preserve the fragile balance of His plan for nature. As the rainbow angels displayed their handiwork, Timothy prayed that mankind would take heed.

November 5, 2004

Wondering Who Will Be Waiting
At Heaven's Gate

I recently received a book for a birthday gift from some special and dear friends. Although it was less than 200 pages, it had a very profound effect on my life.

For anyone who read *Tuesdays With Morrie*, you might be familiar with the work of the author, Mitch Albom. Well, in this new book of his, entitled *The Five People You Meet In Heaven*, Mr. Albom once again writes in a style that is simple to understand, yet deeply thought provoking.

The central figure in the story is a simple, lonely old man who spends his entire life doing the same menial job. He meets with a tragic accident and encounters, upon his arrival into heaven, five different people that he knew in varying degrees when he was on earth.

Once I started reading the book, I found it impossible to put down. And since I read it, I have had difficulty in getting it out of my mind. I could not help but wonder if only five people from my own life meet me, assuming that I make it to heaven, who they might be. Up until this point in my life, I had always assumed that there would be a huge welcoming committee on hand when I ambled into eternity. They would be wearing shiny halos, waving banners and would put me in the express line right up to St. Peter, as trumpets heralded my triumphant arrival.

Would I be met at the entrance to heaven by one of the nuns who taught me in school? I envisioned one of the sisters standing just inside the pearly gates, ruler in hand, asking me why it took so long to arrive and where had I been. She would give me a sheet of sentences to diagram, and forbid me to pass notes and whisper to anyone else during her allotted time with me. Just as I was beginning to think I had landed in hell instead of heaven, she would tell me what a challenge I had been to her and how she saw untapped potential in my active little mind.

Only then would I see her as an educator and a friend, someone that had tried in vain to channel my energy and the constant workings of my brain into something useful and constructive.

Might I find myself in the heavenly presence of a former college classmate whom I had known by name and face only? I would realize that I had never taken the time, or exerted the energy, to get to know their personality or feelings of inadequacy or loneliness because I was too absorbed in my own schedule.

Would I come face to face in the afterlife with a neighbor I never took the time or trouble to visit? Could there be an unknown person, waiting for my arrival into heaven, that had done a good deed for me that I never knew about? That one deed might have affected the entire path that my life had taken.

We all recognize the people in our lives who are the closest to us, the ones upon whom we spend our time and energy. But this book got me to think about the hundreds of people we encounter that we might never think twice about, and how those encounters can influence and affect our thoughts and actions, as well as those we meet along the way.

I recalled a ragged woman standing outside a fast food restaurant. I was in my car, listening to the radio, weary and anxious to place my order at the drive thru window and get home after a long and stress filled day of work.

As she approached my car, I didn't bother to roll down the window, but just ignored her. When I got to the pick-up window, I described the woman I had seen and asked the server if she had gone inside the restaurant. I told her that I regretted my lack of interest, and wanted to offer to buy her dinner. She wasn't anywhere to be found. If this woman is one of the five waiting for me in heaven, I wonder if it will be too late for me to apologize to her.

Thanks, Mr. Albom, for writing a little book that will help me to treat every person that I encounter while I'm on this earth as if they will have the deciding vote on my ticket into heaven. I can only hope and pray that one of them didn't send me an e-mail prayer chain letter, and realize that I was the one who broke it.

Home Sweet Home

FAMILY MATTERS

Chapter

March 4, 1988

THE NEW MOTHERHOOD

I was shocked when my young neighbor came to greet me at her front door. She had just come home from the hospital with her brand new baby girl, the first baby for her and her husband, and I expected to find her frazzled, nervous, and looking very much the part of a new mother.

She was dressed in her "pre-pregnancy" tailored, well fitting slacks, a matching sweater, and leather flat heeled shoes with hose. Her hair was beauty shop fresh, and her makeup was flawless. She wore cologne and jewelry, and her fingernails were manicured and polished to perfection.

"Oh, I'm sorry. I see you must be getting ready to leave for a visit to the doctor's office. I'll come over to see the baby on another day," I told her.

"No, no, I'm not going anywhere. Come on in and see our precious little girl," she responded.

The baby was a true beauty, and instead of an ordinary day gown and booties, she was dressed in a hand smocked gown, with matching satin shoes and lace edged socks. Her nursery was picture perfect, with wicker accessories, antique cradle, and a closet filled with frilly outfits. I knew in my heart that if "Tommy Tippee"® cups were available in sterling silver, this child would certainly have one.

"I really should go, I can tell that you must be expecting company since you are both so dressed up," I told the new mother.

"What makes you think that?" She replied.

"Well, you just look like you're either going somewhere or having company," I explained.

Visions of my own first days home from the hospital after the birth of a new baby came to my mind. The first few days I hobbled around the apartment dressed in my gown and robe. My hair was a sight, and if I managed to wash my face and put on lipstick before my husband got home in the evenings, I felt I had accomplished a major feat. The baby was dressed in an undershirt and diaper after I learned that he could soak through a minimum of 15 cute little outfits before lunch time. By the time I decided I should burn my gowns and robe, I made the shocking discovery that all of my clothes were too tight, (a fact that still plagues me today, some 20 years after the birth of my last child). I resorted to wearing sweat pants and oversized shirts and sweaters of my husbands, and prayed that by the time. I ventured to the doctor's office for my post-natal check up; I wouldn't have to wear a maternity outfit. I went from the spelling of "Arpage" to "Garbage" rather quickly.

"What could be causing a rash on the baby's bottom?", my neighbor asked, jogging my memory from the past back to the present.

After asking if she had used all the used and true methods of diaper rash treatment, I commented that perhaps the baby was allergic to disposable diapers. A look of horror crossed her face, and I realized that the thought of life, without these modern innovations, was unthinkable to her.

Would she not come to know the fragrance of ammonia constantly rising from the now obsolete diaper pail? Would she never have to call a plumber to retrieve two days worth of soiled linen, inadvertently flushed by some unsuspecting visitor? Would she be denied the pleasure of folding, fresh from the outdoor clothesline, those sweet smelling and sun-bleached white rectangular pieces of cloth? What would she use for dishtowels, or dustrags or "burp" pads for her shoulder? How would her baby learn to play "Peepeye" without the benefit of a cloth diaper to pull off her delighted little face?

One week later, I saw the familiar tall, white plastic pail on the front porch of my neighbor's house, awaiting pick up by the diaper service man, and I wondered if I should jot my plumber's telephone number on the back of a card of pink, plastic tipped diaper pins for her future use.

Sept. 12, 1986

School Mournings

*N*ow that summer is ending and parents eagerly escort their off-spring back to the classrooms, I recall the preparations we used to make each day for school.

The very first day of the school year, without fail, my dear husband made the noble effort to prepare the "all American" breakfast to fill those hungry tummies at our house. We'd have bacon, eggs, toast, juice, coffee, and milk. The second morning we were down to toast, bacon, juice, and coffee. By day number three it was 10 extra minutes in the bunk, the kids, Mom as ringmaster, cold cereal, and out of the box toaster pastries to go in the car. The rest of the year deteriorated from that point.

We were never able to locate shoes, shirts with buttons, pants with knees in, matching socks, gym clothes, books or homework assignments. It would have appeared as though some mystical thief had stolen into the house as we slept and made off with all the essentials needed for that particular day. He also took all of the change needed for lunches, and because the school frowns on taking checks in the cafeteria line, piggy banks were ransacked. As none of us are "morning people," there was always a great deal of teeth gnashing, hand wringing, and lectures on responsibility, which are all so delightful to deliver or hear when one first awakens.

I soon learned that test papers and notes were never to be signed on the way out of the door. Usually, the test scores on these hastily presented documents will be equal to, if not less than, your child's age. The day I signed a note agreeing to drive a group of 8-year-old boys on a tour of the police station made me become extremely cautious of my future autographs.

After reading those idealistic magazine articles on getting organized, I attempted to give some of the suggestions a try. I set the table for breakfast the night before, got uniforms laid out in individual stacks, and packed lunches in the refrigerator. I was feeling very efficient until I was awakened in the wee morning hours by the sound of one of the boys in the kitchen. He woke up, gravitated toward the refrigerator, thought he'd missed a meal, and promptly devoured his lunch sitting at the table. I got the wrong pants into their allocated piles and one had on high waters, while another tripped over his brother's too long pants. That ended my organization efforts.

Our water meter, between the hours of 6 a.m. and 7, must have looked like Hoover Dam was coming through, Nobody could shower the night before, all hair had to be freshly washed every morning, so there was considerable scrambling to be first, rather than last, into the shower. Note that these fastidious creatures had to be threatened with a hosing down just a few years prior to the onset of puberty, as they avoided the bathtub like the plague.

It's not that mornings were so bad at our house, but the dog would stay under the bed until she heard the car leave the driveway, then crawl out and beg for a bowl of coffee. When they did depart, they would sometimes tell me that "Sister will put me in detention for a year if I come to school without my homework finished." It was difficult to repress a somewhat wishful sigh.

The thought of leaving home on a school morning always seemed to appeal to me, but I never could find my gym bag either, and the dog begged me to stay around, so I had to give it up as a bad idea.

April 17, 1990

THE VEGGIE CONSPIRACY

*P*erhaps we were to blame for our childrens' strange dietary habits. From the day they graduated from that disgusting mixture of rice cereal, mashed ripe bananas, and baby formula, I found it difficult ... no, impossible, to pretend to eat the small, unappetizing demitasse spoons of strained spinach, sweet potatoes, beets, green peas, squash, or carrots. Somehow it was not too convincing for the baby to see Mom or Dad gag on the very stuff they attempted to feed him. Even "here comes the choo-choo" or "open the door for the airplane" resulted in clamped little lips and spattered walls and floors.

There was no problem wolfing down the plums, pears, bananas, apricots, or peaches, and when they graduated to junior baby food, the meat and potatoes selections became favorites. Table food was readily eaten, beginning with the usual mashed potatoes and cooked ground beef. Once more the green, yellow, and orange items on their dinner plates were passed over and most often wound up on the floor beneath the high chairs. The poor dog hunted in vain for a scrap of meat and refused to eat the rejected vegetables.

Out of the baby days and onto the "meals on wheels," as we drove from one practice, meeting, ball game, or other scheduled event. Ronald McDonald should have been a dependent on our income tax return, as hamburgers and fries became the staple of life. It was embarrassing to take the boys to a cafeteria and see them select fried chicken, and for their "vegetables," mashed potatoes, macaroni and cheese, and rice.

I decided to campaign for vegetables. One rare summer evening, when everyone was going to eat together, I prepared all fresh vegetables — corn, green beans, sliced tomatoes, squash — and cornbread. I sat down at the dinner table, and we said the blessing. I began to eat, and noticed no one else was moving.

"OK, Mom, didn't you forget something?"

"No, I don't think so. Why aren't any of you eating your dinner?" I replied.

My husband chimed in, "Where's the beef?"

Ignoring the fact that he'd be terrific in a hamburger commercial, I advised my disbelieving family that we were not eating enough vegetables, and I was launching a new meal format. There was considerable grumbling and lots of turned up noses, but they managed to eat their dinner.

"Mom, if Dad always tells us, 'eat the meat, cause it cost the most,' and you don't serve meat, will we starve?"

I assured my child that he would not starve from lack of meat, but that we were going to be eating more vegetables. My plan eventually worked, and they began to eat some of the green, yellow and orange "yucky" stuff. They even discovered the joy of a crisp, crunchy salad, which had previously been known as "rabbit food."

Naturally, when they became independently mobile, they convinced me that mushrooms on a pizza would satisfy their daily requirements for vegetables, and I hoped that from time to time they would get a craving for squash casserole or eggplant Parmesan. (I finally resigned myself to the fact that brussels sprouts were never going to be accepted, and okra could only be fried.)

* * * * * * * * * *

In June, 1924, in the town of Milton, Massachusetts, a doting mother held her infant son. Dorothy Walker Bush tried her best to convince her George, as he matured, that he should learn to eat his broccoli.

"Don't you know that unless you eat your green veggies, you'll never grow up to be president?"

Even Mothers can't always be right.

January 4, 1987

GLAD RAGS PECKING ORDER

In the wardrobe of every child, there are three categories of clothing: play clothes, school clothes, and church clothes. In order to understand the criteria for each classification of attire, it is important to describe each of them in detail.

The first variety, play clothes, are sometimes "hand-me-downs" from older siblings in the family. (This gets to be very embarrassing, and expensive, if the next in line is of a different sex.) I didn't realize how many things I had passed down to our youngest son, from two older brothers, until he asked for clothes "with tags on them" as a ninth birthday gift.

It was always appealing to me to pick out the matching sets of pants and knit shirts. With tigers, lions, giraffes, and other animals as logo, it was easy to match them up. They looked so neat and coordinated when I first put them on my children. It was interesting to note that, after the initial wearing, the pants and shirts were never to be seen worn together again. The elephants ended up with giraffes, and the hippos didn't fare well with leopards.

Play clothes, even when put on clean, seemed to attract dirt like a magnet, and no amount of rubbing, scrubbing, or pre-soaking could ever quite remove all the grubbiness they, and their wearers, collected.

School attire, blessedly for my parochial grammar schoolers, was uniforms. When I had to wear them as a student, I despised them, but when the time arrived for my own children to be outfitted in them, I was eternally grateful for this traditional attire. There was one less decision for us to make each morning, and consequently, one less matter for discussion. Picture day was always a nightmare, as they could wear non-uniform clothes, and no matter what was chosen the preceding night at bedtime, it was vetoed by morning, and the choices were rearranged many times the morning of the photo session.

It was wonderful to see, on the first day of every school year, all the students filing into Mass wearing their clean, neat new uniforms, exemplifying all that the word "uniform" connoted. By Christmas break, it was a different story. The boys were wearing trousers with patches reinforcing the knees, buttons missing from their shirts, and shoes that looked as if they had been worn to plow the "back forty." Most of the girls had hems held up by safety pins, and knee socks, with stretched elastic, down around their ankles. By the end of May, the next stop for these poor ragged togs was usually the trash can.

Most closets contain at least one nice, or Sunday, outfit, which magically transforms unkempt little urchins into shiny faced cherubs. When we traveled across the United States with our three sons, in a van, with a platform bed in the back, and a backpacking tent for sleeping accommodations, I thought it would be fun for us to audition for the "Family Feud" television game show. Of course, I had also agreed to go on this Western camping vacation and wasn't in my right mind at the time. I wrote to the show and got a date and time for us to appear while we were in California. I instructed my 4 males to bring a sport coat, nice pants, dress shirt and a tie for our debut. On the appointed morning, they each appeared wearing khaki pants, navy blue blazers white button down shirts and striped ties. With all of them wearing glasses, I could have easily been mistaken for the girl singer in an all boy band. After much grumbling and complaints of not really wanting to go to the audition, I surrendered to the majority rule, and the standard male dress attire was quickly relegated back to suitcases.

There is one article of clothing that seems to encompass all types of need. The youth of America are in uniform, and they love it. The more worn and faded, the better they seem to like it. Levi Strauss has outfitted teenagers for all occasions by their creation of blue denim jeans. Wouldn't it be interesting to discover that they were the invention of someone's mother? Just imagine how many overcoats would be sold.

November 14, 1989

Teenage Wasteland

When the most watched program on television is the city council meeting, there is a problem in the community. The movers and shakers of our fair city have been in turmoil lately, and the citizens are becoming a very vocal, angry mob, ready to lynch any and all governing officials. (Lest anyone suspect that the tone of my article is taking a political overtone, I assure the readers that I am merely pointing out an obvious problem, and feel that I have a perfectly legitimate solution.)

Out of the 29 proposed city dump sites, there seems to be none that will be acceptable. We object to pollutants in our water, soil, and environment. We don't want the huge trucks tearing up our neighborhoods, and no property owner in their right mind wants to see his or her home surrounded by decaying waste.

There is one group that would, I feel, never object to the landfill. They would embrace the idea, and not place one irate telephone call to their councilperson. The tons of waste would be absorbed easily into their environment, and the burden of selecting an appropriate landfill site would be put to rest once and for all.

With an estimated population of around 500,000, it would be reasonable to estimate that at least one fifth of this total number would be between the ages of 12 and 25. If all the garbage were evenly divided among the rooms of 100,000 of these teenagers and young adults, I will personally guarantee that it would never be detected by the inhabitants of the selected sites. Anyone who has ever lived with a person in this age category can certainly identify with my observations.

The room of a person in the aforementioned age group is, without a doubt, the most disgusting place on the face of the earth. Live creatures have been known to disappear forever in the room of a teenager. Parents wisely refrain from entering these sanctuaries, family pets vacate the bunk beds for more sanitary surroundings, and only the bravest of souls would dare to attempt to clean one. It is the final resting place for damp bath towels, soft drink cans, pizza delivery boxes, crickets, and automobile transmission parts. If you suspect that something you value may have wound up in "that room," pray that it has very little monetary value, and purchase a new one rather than destroying your nervous system.

When company comes for a visit, it is best to board up the room, and place a quarantine sign on the door.(Hopefully, your guests won't remember that leprosy is not too prevalent in the Southern United States and will not question your motives.) My mother once came for a surprise visit, entered the grandsons' bedrooms, and hyperventilated for 30 minutes before she left in a state of shocked dismay.

"How often do you vacuum and dust their rooms?" she asked, her voice faltering.

"Mother, get serious. I think shovel and fumigate would be more in order ... Yes ma'am, I know that I wasn't raised to live like that ... No ma'am, I won't ever make you go in there again ... Yes ma'am, the quarantine sign is merely a joke ... Yes ma'am, they have had all their shots, and they don't have head lice — they shampoo their hair 14 times every day."

When they run out of clean clothes, they dig out enough from under the beds, off the desk and chairs, and recycle the body odors. Somehow or another, they manage to find almost every item they stockpile in these rooms, and no matter what clutters the room, the stereo speakers are the only unobstructed and unadorned article in the area. Perhaps it is the loud decibels of music that destroys the nests of live creatures who would otherwise thrive and multiply in these habitats.

Not only would distributing the city's refuse in these rooms solve a lot of problems, the need for garbage trucks could also be eliminated. Ever look for something lost in the back seat of a jeep?

September 27, 1988

SCHEDULE FROM HELL

*A*fter years of unsuccessfully trying to juggle all the various activities and commitments of an active household, I decided to post a calendar for all the family to write in their daily schedule. I got a nice big poster board, measured off large squares, wrote the days of the week across the top, and taped it to the kitchen wall, tied a felt tip pen to a thumb tack, and broke the news at dinner time.

"In case anyone wants to know what the big poster board on the wall is, I'd like to explain," I began.

Suspicious looks were exchanged around the table, elbows were jammed into ribs, and eyes rolled backward, indicating that whatever I said next was not going to be taken too seriously.

I fearlessly continued, "We need to be more organized. It seems that we are always in the car, on the way to or from something, and we dash in the house, change into the next uniform or outfit, jump back into the car, and head out once more. I feel as if the station wagon is our permanent residence, and home is just a place to visit." Blank stares met my gaze after I finished speaking and the rare silence in the room was noticeable

I asked that each family member, (dogs and cats excluded), write the activities for each upcoming weekday on Sunday, so that I could arrange my schedule, and possibly fit in some time away from the steering wheel. In order to demonstrate, I began by writing in on Monday, "Dentist, check-ups, 3:45 p.m." and on Friday, "Vet, puppy shots, 4 p.m." They quickly caught on to the idea, and I left them to appreciate the beauty and peace that would result from our newly found organizational plan.

On Monday morning, I went in the kitchen to check the daily roster, and was horrified to see what was in store for me the current week. My calendar read as follows:

Monday — 3-3:30 p.m., patrol duty; 3-4 p.m., ball practice; 3:30-5 p.m.

birthday party at skating rink; 3:45 p.m. dentist check-ups, 4:30 p.m., pick up suit at cleaners before closing.

Tuesday — 3-3:30 p.m. guitar lesson; 3-4 p.m. Cub Scout meeting (Mom, bring two dozen cookies and punch); 3:30-5 p.m. ball game; 6 p.m. — Out of town clients for dinner out (wear make-up and no sweatsuits, please).

Wednesday — 3-4:30 p.m. class field trip to downtown library. (Mom drive 10 students); 3-5 p.m., ball game away; 3:30-5 p.m., piano lesson; 7:30 p.m., surprise birthday party for next-door neighbor (bring covered dish).

Thursday — 3-4:30 p.m. ball practice; 3:30-5 p.m., altar boy picnic (Mom, bring four dozen chocolate chip cookies, and some big Cokes); 3:15-4:30 p.m., Boy Scout meeting; 7:30 p.m. Home and School meeting (Bring three dozen brownies on silver tray).

Friday — 3-4 p.m., need to go to barbershop for haircuts; 3:30-5 p.m., ball practice; 3:15-4:30 p.m., play practice; 4 p.m., vet (puppy shots); 7:30-10 p.m., seventh grade dance — gym (Mom and Dad chaperone and bring four dozen cupcakes).

Saturday — 8 a.m-ball game away (40 miles). Arrive in uniform by 7:30 a.m.; 9 a.m. — Oil change for car, 10:30 a.m. — Rabies clinic for all dogs and cats; 11:15 a.m. — Out of town visitors arrive for weekend of sight-seeing; noon — Take elderly aunt to grocery; 2 p.m. — Baby shower for co-worker.

I made one last entry before discarding the calendar and replacing it with the car keys and a city map: "Disregard all written notices previously listed."

Some things are better left to chance, I learned.

April 15, 1992

UNIFORMED RESPONSE

A controversy occurred among parents and students of the public school systems. Should uniforms be worn? The opponents find valid reasons to dismiss the idea as a bad one, while those supporting the notion continue to present positive reasons for the city councils to rule in their favor.

As a former uniform wearer, as well as the parent of three formerly little uniformed students, I feel qualified to give testimony to both pros and cons. It didn't matter if your family drove a brand new Cadillac or a 20-year-old jalopy, you wore the same clothes as everyone in the school. Your father could be a wealthy businessman, or your mother could be the primary support of the family, everyone dressed alike at school. You could be short, tall, skinny, or fat, and the uniforms were only bigger or smaller according to individual needs. There was no frantic shopping for school clothes every September, just place your order, list your measurements, write a check and wait for the uniforms to arrive.

I've seen attractive, well made uniforms on students. I was not fortunate enough to fall into that category. The uniform I wore, from kindergarten until the day I finally graduated and burned it, (I firmly believe that it was the same one and just grew with me), was the most unattractive creation ever made. It was a navy blue jumper, got shiny where it was sat on, wrinkled badly, and was made from a gabardine material, imported from the loom of Satan. Beneath these shapeless jumpers, we wore white V-necked cotton blouses. For dress up occasions, like May procession and the Christmas carol program, we wore long sleeve blouses, and if we were cold natured, a navy blue sweater completed our ensemble. Because I attended an all girl school, it was not necessary to have coordinating unattractive male attire.

We were taught that our uniforms made us representatives of our school. We knew if we did anything to discredit it, we were not only endangering our own reputation, but that of the academy. It was easy to spot us in public and we

63

attracted curious stares and lots of whispered speculation from observers. I certainly don't think that any self-respecting young man, in his right mind, would have dared to cast a second admiring glance in our directions.

After graduation, I got to shop for a college wardrobe, and I came home and laid everything out to look at another time. I selected sweaters, skirts, dresses, and absolutely nothing navy blue. After arriving on campus, I soon learned the most difficult course I was to encounter: getting my clothes ready for the day. After a lifetime of knowing what I was going to wear every morning and not having to make major decisions before breakfast, I was in a state of shock. If my grey plaid skirt was clean, the white sweater was dirty, and if my yellow blouse needed a button and I was running late for an eight o'clock class and couldn't find a single safety pin, the day didn't get off to a very good start. I found myself wanting to resurrect the navy blue jumper and start a new fashion trend on campus.

When the time came for me to outfit my own children in their school uniforms, I welcomed the chance to not have to make decisions about their daily attire. At one time, they wore striped vests and looked very much like waiters, but at least all their friends were wearing the same strange clothing and nobody got laughed at. By the time Christmas rolled around, the fall uniform purchases were looking pretty shoddy and worn at the knees, so usually new pants were ordered before they returned to classes in January. Lots of patches were utilized to make the outfits serviceable for the remainder of the school year, and sometimes the cat or dog had to give up their sleeping nest so it could be thrown into the dryer and worn to school.

Once we were free from the obligatory wearing of uniforms, we were able to choose the type of clothes we wore. I recall, however, that leisure suits were in style for men, and miniskirts were being worn by women (even those that shouldn't). Are we any different from the military, medical personnel, airline employees, public transportation workers, or scouts who utilize uniforms every day? Look around us at the teenagers in blue jeans, the executives in their suits and ties, and the suburbanites in jogging suits and tennis shoes. Uniforms in different patterns and colors.

In wearing uniforms, we may have all appeared the same, but perhaps we got the opportunity to really see the individual for what he or she was. Maybe the outward appearance became so unimportant to us that we came to know and value each person for their unique personality, character, and talents.

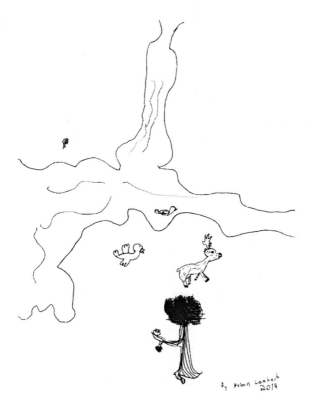

THE GRASS MIGHT NOT ALWAYS BE GREENER

Chapter

January 26, 1998

Just An Old Tree Branch?

*I*t had once been a living part of a magnificent tree, and provided shelter for squirrels and birds. In the springtime, it had produced buds that, with the warmth of the sun and the dampness from showers, became leaves.

During the summer, it had helped to provide shade and protection from the heat of the day, and in the evenings, the slightest hint of breeze would cause its leaves to flutter. It wasn't large enough to support a swing or a hammock, and really even too small to accommodate a bird's nest, but each year it grew a little bigger.

With the crisp autumn weather, the leaves had turned brilliant shades of red, orange, and gold before they withered and fell to the ground. It had withstood countless storms that had threatened to remove it from the tree, and repeated nature's life cycle over many seasons.

Now it was a fallen branch, a casualty of winter, lying lifeless, broken off from the tree that had once nurtured it. It would be run over by the lawn mower in a couple of months, broken into smaller sticks and raked up to be hauled away as trash, or used to start a campfire.

No longer beautiful or productive, it had served its purpose, and now it lay in the back yard, ugly and devoid of life. No one would ever again look at it with admiration.

Bright, active, and enthusiastic, eager for new adventures and ideas, she was a joy to watch and to be around. She was busy searching for the perfect shape and size for her project. Every one she found was either too big, too small or not the right shape. Maybe this wasn't such a good idea, after all, she thought, ready to abandon her plan. She had been looking in the yard for a long time, and was beginning to grow tired of her search.

As she climbed the steps, her eyes caught sight of something on the ground. She ran back down the steps and across the yard to the spot where the branch was lying. It was just the right size and shape. She eagerly snatched it up and headed for the house, wondering how she had overlooked it before. She was very careful not to break it as she laid it on newspaper that had been spread out on the kitchen table.

The table was littered with construction paper, scissors, crayons, paste, glitter, yarn, and paint. After the paint was applied to the branch, it gleamed white, as it had when it used to be covered with the winter snow. It was allowed to dry, and then set into a styrofoam chunk that was imbedded in the bottom of a flowerpot. The first part of the transformation was complete; now it was ready to be decorated.

She painstakingly traced around the shapes and carefully cut out each one. Next she colored them with her crayons and printed names on each one. As a final step, glitter and lengths of yarn were glued to every paper ornament, and then hung from the limbs of the branch. It was finished at last. Her tree was a beautiful sight indeed, and each Valentine heart that dangled from it bore the name of someone she loved very much.

There was one each for her parents, sister, grandparents, aunts, and uncles, cousins, and her two cats. She thought it was the best tree she had ever seen, and she bet that nobody else in the first grade would have anything as beautiful as this.

The branch that had seemed too small had fallen just in time to become a lovely Valentine symbol of a little girl's love for her family.

May 31, 1988

NOT A FLOWER CHILD

Each summer I vow that I'll never put out bedding plants again, and each year I see the petunias, marigolds, pansies, and impatiens in their glorious bright colors, and I forget my promise. I see the beautiful flower beds, and hanging baskets in other yards, and I attempt to create the same setting on my own turf.

I lug the bag of potting soil out of the garage, get my pots and baskets all lined up, don my gardening gloves, and begin the traditional search for my garden tools. It would seem the small potting shovels are multi-purpose implements at our house; they are used to stir paint, anchor camping tents, work on automobile engines, as a paperweight for homework, and a pet food scoop, (I still haven't figured out how one of them was used in the refrigerator, and perhaps that's just as well that I don't). After I finally locate some semblance of a digging utensil, I begin my project.

The dirt is piled in to each container, and then I carefully plant each little blossom securely in the rich soil mixture. I realize as I'm planting that all of these posies must be placed well out of range of our riding lawn mower, for the head gardener, better known as my spouse, mows anything in his path. I have, in years past, hidden small clumps of blooming plants in remote corners of the yard, only to have him hunt them out with his mini-tractor and "accidentally" cut them down in their prime. I have learned to hang the plants out of his way, or put them on concrete, in defense of horticulture.

After dutifully watering, fertilizing, pinching, pruning, and weeding my little blossoms, I am rewarded with a couple of weeks of their presentable blooms, and then they begin to wither, droop, become barren as the desert, and realize that my green thumb is merely the result of mold and mildew. (Perhaps the kindest thing ever done for a plant, in my care, was to mow it down before I got a chance to submit it to a slow, agonizing demise.)

I move them into the sun, out of the sun, morning light, moonlight, and total eclipse. I feed them, talk to them, show them pictures of what they are supposed to look like, and promise to nurture their offspring buds, all without results. I try ignoring them, coaxing them, and threatening them, and still they just sit there, looking like undernourished, neglected waifs. My impatiens become impatient, my petunias are the pits, my begonias are woe be gone, and my salvia, unsalvageable.

The great huge vases of cut flowers that are seen adorning the homes of others won't ever be possible for me to create, but I have discovered a lovely plant that I have not been able to destroy. The leaves stay green year round, it does not need watering, sunlight, fertilizer, or rich potting soil for its roots. It has an indefinite lifespan, and it will never attract insects to its leaves. The red blossoms are robust, full and don't wilt from the effects of too little or too much rainfall. It will never need repotting, mulching, or pruning, and frost won't kill it if I forget to bring it in on a cool evening,

I don't know who invented the silk geranium, but I'm willing to bet it was someone who understood my dilemma.

May 8, 1989

MOWED DOWN

When springtime arrived and the grass began to come back to life, it always was understood that Mom doesn't do lawns. With a house full of male inhabitants, I felt it was never going to be necessary for me to be on the business end of a power mower. It always worked, and for years the sole contribution I made to lawn work was to set out some ice water for the laborers, and sweep the sidewalk when the work was completed. It seemed to be a great arrangement; they told me when their favorite shirt needed ironing, when we were out of chips or ice cream, or when the available funds in their sparse bank accounts didn't quite cover their "expenses," and I would point out that the grass was certainly getting out of hand. The first paying job that any of our sons had was cutting grass for the neighbors, and the legacy was handed down from one to the other for several seasons.

As the boys grew older, and so did we, they became less available for lawn work, and my husband became the "grounds keeper." He came to enjoy the work, and took pride in his ability to make our yard attractive. To compliment his riding mower, he purchased a "lawn sweeper," which trailed along behind the mower, giving the yard a clean appearance.

After major surgery prohibited him from any strenuous work, and despite my inexperience, I tackled the yard. After several hours of detailed explanations about the working parts of a lawn mower, and repeated cautions concerning the dangers involved, he felt I was ready to solo with the small mower. Starting it proved to be more of a problem than either of us had anticipated, but once we got past that minor difficulty, I was making paths across the front lawn. He pointed out that it might be better to set a pattern, rather than zigzagging in the random fashion I had established, and I made every effort to find one that seemed attractive.

Realizing that the worst part was over, and I could ride on the big mower to cut the back yard, I donned my sun visor, headphone radio, and grabbed my plastic water bottle from the refrigerator, prepared to enjoy the remainder of my task.

"You can't hear me telling you how to cut, with that radio on your ears," my foreman shouted out from his lawn chair.

Suppressing a smirk, I promised that I'd keep the volume very low. After all, how difficult could this be?

After a jack rabbit start, which caused me to spill my water, lose my visor, and put the headphones around my neck, I was bouncing through ruts, dodging our dogs, running over tree branches, and wondering how in the world anybody could ever manage to smile and wave when they were on one of these horrid machines.

"Shift your weight," I heard him call to me.

He neglected to say which direction, and I fought to keep both the mower and my remaining dignity intact. I forgot how to put it in reverse, and got stuck next to the fence, then I got too close to the apple tree and left my sunglasses embedded in its lower branches.

It was hard to tell which looked worse after I finished; the lawn or me. I prayed for drought so I'd never have to do this wretched job again, and after the good Lord denied that selfish plea, He saw fit to send an angel one evening who spared me from my horrible fate again. (I later discovered that my "angel" lived next door, and I forever bless my good fortune.)

Our eldest son came over to cut the lawn a couple of weeks later, but knowing that the dreaded grass was going to continue to grow all summer, I wondered if our dogs could learn to get along with a couple of goats.

September 5, 1990

Growing Tomatoes Like Guerilla Warfare

*J*uicy, red, and picture pretty, I thought, as I sliced through the succulent outer skin of my very own homegrown tomatoes. The waning days of summer seemed to cry out for tall, frosty pitchers of iced tea, cornbread, and the last remnants of the season's vegetables to grace the supper table. What better meal could there be than fresh corn on the cob, squash, beans, and sliced tomatoes? Ah, Ronald, if you could only serve a McVeggie dinner, your arches could be platinum instead of gold.

Early this spring, I succumbed to a special sale on tomato plants, and bought eight of them for $4. Not a bad investment, I reasoned, for an entire three months of summer eating pleasure. I had friends that froze their summer harvest surplus, and enjoyed them in soup, chili, and stew throughout the barren winter. I'd have a whole freezer filled with tasty tomatoes that I had grown, and I'd savor the memories of my summer garden while I watched the snow cover the frozen ground.

My plants were very small when I planted them, (for 50 cents apiece, it was assumed that the gardener would work tirelessly for a productive crop yield).

"Be sure you set them in a piece of newspaper before you put them in the ground, and leave a little bit of it sticking up above the surface," was the advice of a long time successful tomato planter acquaintance.

"Why?" I dared to ask.

"Lord, don't you know about the cutworms, honey?"

"Cutworms?" I repeated, picturing large, vicious, hungry creatures with razor sharp fangs attacking my tiny plants while I slept.

"Well, you just put that newspaper around those plants like I told you, and those cutworms will leave them alone, I guarantee you."

After the untimely demise of one of my "Better Boys" beneath the whirling whip of the weedeater, I bought cages for the tomatoes. Looking at the diminutive plants, firmly embedded in *USA Today* money pages, surrounded by huge wire cone shaped cages, I wondered if they would ever reach the top rung.

"They need Miracle Gro®," a neighbor told me as I watered my struggling little crop.

"Oh, sure, I know that. In fact I already gave them a dose, but thanks for your concern," I replied.

I searched the shelves at the garden shop for Miracle Gro®, and waited until dark could hide me from the watchful eyes of my green thumbed neighbor. I mixed the fertilizer, according to package directions, and fully expected to awaken the next morning to a modern day re-enactment of Jack and the Beanstalk. It was several days before I noticed several tiny yellow flowers on the healthier looking plants. I celebrated with another Miracle Gro® cocktail for my plants.

They grew, and grew, and grew. I propped their branches to keep them from breaking, and tied nylon stockings to the fence for support. I learned how to "sucker" the plants. They extended far beyond the confines of their cages, and overlapped each other in their small plot of ground. The green tomatoes began to turn pink, and I eagerly awaited the first pick of the crop. It was beautiful, and as I reached to take it off the vine, I was horrified to discover that the birds had beaten me to it.

I erected a scarecrow, and they lit on his head to reach the tomatoes. I put up aluminum pie pans, and the blasted winged marauders used them as toys, banging into them as they swooped down on my coveted tomatoes. I put up a birdbath, thinking that if they could get water, perhaps they would leave the tomatoes alone. They brought the remnants of the tomatoes into the birdbath. A rubber snake, I was told, would definitely scare the thieves away. The snake did nothing to frighten the birds, but did manage to create a slight problem for one of our visiting sons, who was unaware of my decoy.

I put out metallic pinwheels, (the kind small children love to hold out car windows), and mesh netting. My tomato plants resembled a small fortress, but still the enemy managed to invade.

At last count, I had gotten 12 tomatoes from my plants, three of them in the freezer as a memento, and the remaining nine, I estimated cost seven dollars each. Next summer, I think I'll switch to bird watching.

January 6, 1992

WHY FLORISTS EXIST

Some people have the knack for gardening and it shows in their plant windows and well landscaped yards. While I love the beauty of fresh flowers, and long to have giant vases filled with them all through the house, I never have been able to cultivate a very healthy crop of blossoms. I weed, fertilize, water, and struggle to keep plants alive, but they wither, mold, droop, and refuse to adequately reward my efforts.

You've seen African violets, I'm sure. They have fuzzy green leaves and lots of little pink, purple or white flowers. They are houseplants that sit on coffee tables of certain fortunate individuals, where they grow to be the average size of Mrs. King Kong's bridal bouquet. I have been given many seemingly healthy African violets in the past, but these poor unfortunate plants know the moment they enter my house they are doomed for death. The blooms begin to disappear and the plants shrivel immediately.

"Put them in a window," I am advised by one violet expert.

I comply with her suggestions, only to have the once beautiful plant resemble a box turtle retreating into its fuzzy shell.

"Don't pour water onto the leaves, just fill the dish and let it drink from its roots," my mother used to admonish.

"Talk to your plants," I am advised. I tell them that I love them, and they must eat all their plant food to grow big and strong. I promise them new pots to live in if they will have little baby flowers for me to show off to all my friends. They pay about as much attention to me as my children do when I attempt to speak to them. There is something very unsettling about a plant turning its head when it hears the sound of my voice.

I begin to feel very much like the unsuspecting caretaker from "Little Shop of Horrors," as I try to nurture ailing plants. I follow dozens of helpful tips, including fertilizer sticks, florescent lights, warm water, and repotting. I become nauseated when I visit homes where the "all I do is water it every once in a while" approach results in show quality plants.

Thinking that perhaps my lack of success was just with indoor species, I decided to try my luck with the great outdoors and plant some roses. (African violets have an underground network and they passed the command to the Kamikaze rose bushes, "prepare to give up your lives to this hopeless amateur.") I battled black spots, mildew, aphids, and fungus. I sprayed, mulched, pruned, watered, dusted, fed, and transplanted. Instead of beautiful rose bouquets, I managed to grow dried potpourri on the bushes.

After the colorless days of winter, I was eager to introduce some bright patches of color into our bare lawn. With my trusty shovel in gardening gloved hand, trays of healthy bedding plants, potting soil, and seed packets in the new red wheelbarrow, I embarked on my springtime gardening venture, determined to overcome my bad luck with living green things.

Ignoring their sharp, earthy odor I put several bright pink geraniums in clay pots on the patio. In the hanging plastic pots, I carefully nestled little individual clumps of impatiens into the rich soil mixture. The white petunias cascaded over the edges of their baskets, and the orange and yellow marigolds formed a colorful border at the base of the lamp post by the front walk. I got out the old pitchfork, hoe, and rake and spent one entire afternoon planting flower seeds in a small patch of our yard. I surveyed my labors with a great sense of satisfaction and decided that perhaps my brown thumb had finally turned green.

Why didn't someone warn me about what blackberry winter can do to outdoor plants?

GARDEN MULCH:
YOU CAN'T EVER HAVE TOO MUCH

A yard is defined as the ground around, or next to, a building: A lawn is land covered with grass, kept closely mowed, especially around a house. If these definitions are taken in the literal sense, a front "yard" might be bare of trees, grass, and flowers, but a back "lawn" would be a thick green carpet of well manicured grass. We had used our yard for years, but were finally attempting to cultivate it into a lawn.

The bare spots left behind after the swing sets, slides, sand boxes, clubhouse, jungle jim, bicycles, wagons, dogs, lemonade stands, car ramps, and wading pools, finally have grass on them. There are no more oil puddle residues, no deflated footballs, tire rims, or rusting engine parts lying on the ground. We no longer stumbled over broken screwdrivers, aluminum bats, tackle boxes, or bait buckets, and the lawn mower blades no longer spit out shag golf balls, popsicle sticks, and pieces of car stereo wiring.

Our sizeable shrubs, left dead from the freeze a few winters ago, were replaced with some landscaping. The once small replacement bushes finally grew to a respectable size, but the mulch around them needed to be replaced. In years past, we lugged huge bags of mulch from the garden center; only to discover that the contents of one of those oversized bags only fills a space the size of a dinner plate. One fateful year, deciding to save money, time, and labor, my husband found a place where we could fill the back of our pick-up truck with pitch black mulch, for a very reasonable price.

After a hot morning of working in the yard, (soon to become a lawn), we were dirty, sweaty, and smelling less than fragrant. My husband had a day's unshaven growth of beard, and I, without benefit of make-up, looked like a rejected candidate for a total makeover. We found a tarpaulin and some elastic tie downs in the garage and threw them in our clean little half ton pick-up truck. I pulled a faded baseball cap over my nasty hair, and in grass stained old sneakers, soiled teeshirts, and muddy shorts, we took off for our destination.

Long before we saw what we wanted, we smelled it. The unmistakable odor of damp mulch filled the air for the entire block. As we turned into the driveway, we saw the huge mulch mounds. While he went into the office to pay for our intended purchase, I wondered how long it would take to fill the back of our truck, and how much longer I could endure the aroma. With bill of sale in hand, we took a right turn at the first tan mountain, and took our place in line to wait for our mulch.

"I told the guy I just needed a yard of the stuff, but he said the truck could handle a yard and a half, and it was only $12 more, so I said OK," my bargain hunter husband announced.

Not only was our shiny, red small pick-up out of place amidst the other large rusted, dented ones, but I immediately noticed that we were overdressed for the occasion; we were also the only customers without a shovel, rake, or a contractors' wheelbarrow. A huge bulldozer took a giant bite out of Mulch Mountain, pivoted like a wounded dinosaur, and dumped the contents into the first truck in line. The mulch filled the truck bed, and spilled over onto the ground. The driver just ahead of us moved into loading position, and the giant scoop spilled its contents onto the cab, windows, and wheels, as well as the truck bed. As we pulled forward, I felt the truck immediately weighed down, as if Godzilla had stepped on us. We quickly drove out of the way, and pulled over to check our purchase. It was piled high, above the rear window of the cab, and we stretched the tarp to cover most of the smelly black contents. The back of the truck barely cleared the ground, and we very slowly drove home, checking the tarp every mile of the way.

We backed the truck into the yard, and began shoveling the mulch around the shrubs. Two hours later, the shrubs were deeply surrounded, and the mulch was still piled high in the back of the truck. Four hours later, all the trees had a wide ring of black mulch around their bases, and the mulch supply was still plentiful. Six hours later, after we had covered every available area of the lawn with mulch, it grew dark and we contemplated parking the truck on the street, with a "free mulch" sign in it.

The next day we convinced my husband's brother and his wife that their yard would look wonderful with some nice mulch. By the end of his second full day of mulching, as he swept out the back of the truck, someone realized that he got much more than he bargained for "for only $12 more".

July 17, 1995

BLACKBERRY PICKIN' TIME

"**B**lackberries — $3.00 per pint." They looked appealing I must admit, but it would take at least $9 worth of those wonderful juicy berries to satisfy my summer craving. On our regular walk that evening, I mentioned the high cost of blackberries, and my friend generously offered to take us to their property "out in the country," to pick our own harvest.

"Better bring lots of insect repellent," she cautioned. "Those chiggers thrive in the blackberry patch, and they'll eat you alive."

Born and raised in Brooklyn, New York, my husband had never seen a blackberry outside of a jar of jam, much less understand the feeding habits of those wonderful, microscopic, red, little Southern mites called chiggers. He always referred to any insect bite as a "mosquito," and even though they loved to dine on him, he was blissfully ignorant of those belly button loving, pesky chiggers.

"We're going blackberry picking," I bragged to a former neighbor.

"Well, you'll get eaten alive by the chiggers," she admonished.

"Oh, I've taken care of that problem. We're going to douse ourselves in repellent and cover up every square inch of exposed skin."

"What about the snakes?"

"Excuse me, but it sounded like you just said something about 'snakes' ... I must have misunderstood you."

"Un-uh, honey, you didn't misunderstand me, I said S-N-A-K-E-S, you know, those slithering creatures without legs."

"Snakes, as in serpent? Like the devil that was the downfall of Adam and Eve in the Garden of Eden? (Was there a blackberry patch there?)"

"Yes, my dear, snakes love to hide in thick brush, and believe you me, the blackberry patch is a perfect home for them."

Outfitted in long pants, long sleeve shirts, hats, and reeking of insect repellent, we arrived "in the country." With buckets on our arms, and the early afternoon sun beating down on our heads, we ventured a few yards from the house, down a little hill, and approached the bramble bushes laden with wild blackberries. Looking down for serpents, and feeling imaginary chiggers crawling up my sleeves, I frantically pulled berries. Within a few minutes, I was caught in the thorny branches, and could not tell if the red stains on my fingers were from scratches or the juice from blackberries.

I called out to my husband, and the couple we were with. They were all busy filling their buckets, and asked how many I had. I glanced down for the first look at my efforts, and was surprised that the bottom of the bucket was barely covered.

I imagined that it would have been at least half full, since we had been at it for almost an hour. I met up with my husband, confiscated the contents of his bucket, and combined them into one. We still only had about one third of the bucket filled. The perspiration began trickling from my well shaded head and found its way into the corners of my eyes, stinging them and making it difficult to see. I wiped them with my red stained shirt sleeve, and continued searching for more berries, ever mindful of any crawling critters in the vicinity.

I can't remember who decided that it was quitting time, but I do know that I was the first one sitting in the shade, sipping a glass of cool water. Our bucket was still not filled to the half way point, but we were content to call it a day, and head back to the "city," for the luxury of air conditioning and a cool shower.

The blackberry cobblers were delicious, and we wore our chigger bites proudly to show for our hard work. When I asked my husband how he enjoyed his first blackberry picking experience, he pointed out that it was also his last.

After I added up the cost of one large can of insect repellent, two hopelessly stained shirts, and several bottles of clear nail polish to treat the inevitable chigger bites, I decided that $3 was a small price to pay for a pint of blackberries picked by someone else.

April 22, 1997

Planters' Paradox

*M*arch entered like a lion, with flooding, storms, and cold weather, but exited, true to the old adage, like a lamb.

After a fairly mild Tennessee winter, it seemed that spring had arrived early, as temperatures climbed near the 70 degree mark and windows were opened to allow fresh warm breezes to erase the stale remnants of winter from the house. The grass grew greener and taller by the hour, and the familiar drone of hibernating power lawn mowers began to permeate the neighborhood. Crocuses, tulips and daffodils slowly poked their tops from beneath the cold ground, reaching towards the warmth of sunshine. The trees, which had been so bare and stark against the skies of winter, began to sprout green leaves and buds.

The cycle of nature kicked in full force, as the promise of spring rebirth replaced the dormant state of winter. Surely, it was time now to pack away the turtleneck shirts, boots, sweaters, coats, and snow shovels, and pull out shorts, sandals, bathing suits, sun visors, and gardening tools.

I eyed the scraggly remains of last year's glorious petunias, now dead spindly sticks, still firmly entrenched in the potting soil of the hanging planters on our deck. Perhaps I left them there in the hopes that they would regenerate much like the trees and flowers always did. I didn't have the heart to toss them, but now it was time to give them, and all the other pots and planters some new foliage for spring. I made a list of colors and varieties to purchase, and penciled, "buy bedding plants" into my date book for the end of March.

Overnight, the weather changed. The almost forgotten chill of winter blasted in through the screen of the open bathroom window, warning me that it was too early to plant. The windows were quickly shut, the heat turned up, and spring retreated for a bit longer. This was redbud winter, I was told by those who seemed to know. I reluctantly folded the garden shopping list, and pulled a folded blanket from the linen closet to replace on the bed. As I retrieved a turtleneck front the winter storage chest, and listened to the March winds blowing fiercely, it seemed as though they were trying to forestall the oncoming of a rival season.

The Farmer's Almanac and my Grandmas, all invaluable sources of all sorts of information, warned not to plant before Mothers' Day, but that seemed so far away while in early April. Surely, the danger of frost had passed, I thought, as I observed the forsythias spraying the landscape with their cheerful yellow branches. Ah, but next came "dogwood winter," which was followed by "blackberry" and "locust." Each time I thought it was safe to try my green thumb, I got reminded that it really is not nice to fool Mother Nature because she is a very unpredictable lady, especially when she's getting ready for her showiest production of the year.

The azalea bushes came alive in April, loaded with lush white blooms, but had to be covered several nights to protect them from the frost. I moved the geraniums from the basement sun room out onto the patio, and within a few days, heeding the weather forecast for another cold snap, they were hauled back in to escape certain death.

On a warm April Sunday, anxious to get on with the business of planting, and certain now that all the Southern "winters" were finished, I made a trip to the garden center. Weaving my way in, past the crowded checkout lines, I discovered the shelves had been ransacked, and all that remained were a few sickly looking little pots of bedding plants. The remaining impatiens looked ... well, impatient to survive, and the mountains of bagged potting soil were quickly dwindling to one mere pallet, as droves of customers filled their pickup trucks and minivans with their purchases.

I'll heed the old time honored warnings and restrain myself forevermore until the second Sunday in May to put in my annuals, but has anyone ever heard of a "petunia winter?"

FITNESS REDEFINED

Chapter

December 21, 1986

HOLIDAY HIPS ARE BACK

The last crumbs of the Christmas coconut cake have been thrown out. No more cheese balls, dip and chips, sausage pinwheels, or guacamole surprises. The last "perfect gift" has been exchanged, and all those near extinct boxes for presents have been stored in an out of the way place, until next year. The tree, once so beautiful, is now shedding its' needles into the carpet, and the red and green candles sit lopsided in their seasonal holders. This Christmas now joins the ghosts of other past Christmases, and the inevitable January "blahs" make their unwelcome appearance into our lives.

It would be depressing enough to look out the window, and see brown dormant lawns, punctuated by bare limbed trees, but as I gaze out my window, I see a reflected image of too many parties, cookies, and "fa, la, laing". The weight I've struggled so valiantly to lose has found me, once again. I have read that fat cells don't disappear, they merely deflate, like tiny balloons, and wait to be plumped up again. Mine, apparently, have gotten the go-ahead from somewhere in my metabolism, for they are inflating themselves at a surprisingly rapid rate, transforming themselves into strange shaped balloon animals beneath my skin.

The best way to win this battle of the bulge, I've learned from my many sources on weight loss, is to exercise. It sounds so simple, but is so very complicated. Let's face it, exercise, per se, is a very boring way to spend ones' free time. It seems that, at this particular era of my life, walking is the most sensible and result-producing form of activity to burn up all those nasty little calories. There is something very unappealing about setting out for a walk by oneself, and although my trio of canines eagerly attempts to accompany me, it is not the sort of companionship I desire.

It seems as though there are all sorts of obstacles to overcome, if one desires to be physically fit. The weather is a big factor in deciding if I should leave the sheltered confines of my home, and set out on a jaunt around the neighborhood. In the winter months, it is really too cold, or too dark, or too rainy, so that gets us right into spring and summer. I have hay fever in the spring, and it really is too hot in the summer. It is so much easier to become a "couch potato" and watch other brave folks participate in exercise. I always did think it was a spectator sport, anyway.

I have a limited membership in a local health club; the result of a bargain priced promotional advertisement. When I first joined, I envisioned myself looking like Jane Fonda. Now that I have attempted that lofty ambition, and failed, I think a more realistic model would have been her father, Henry. My exercise togs left a lot to be desired. The accepted attire, for all those well toned, firm, young bodies was shiny tights, coordinating leotard, and matching leg warmers and sweat band. My grey sweat pants, with the pink nylon drawstring, faded concert tee shirt,(which lay unclaimed for a year in the bottom of my laundry basket), and my generic tennies really seemed a bit frumpy. There were mirrors all over the walls, and I had a difficult time keeping my head down to prevent myself from getting hopelessly depressed.

As I now find myself in desperate need of an aerobic activity. I think I'll opt for an exercise bike, which I'll place in front of the television. At least no one will see me, and I can sing along with the Jane Fonda tape.

January 23, 1988

OF SWEAT AND SPUDS

*W*atch out, all you Shriners, Elks, and Knights of Columbus. A new organization is having a convention in Lincolnwood, Illinois, that could possibly attract more members than any other group in the history of fraternal organizations. The Associated Press reports that, "hundreds of television addicts, including a Chicago Bears lineman" converged to bask in the warm knowledge that they are not alone in their favorite pastime. They are among the growing numbers of leisure lovers who attended the first National Couch Potato Convention.

Yuppies were formerly the "in" group, but being a couch potato is so much simpler. All it requires is a lack of energy, no ambition, and a comfortable lounging spot where a television set and nourishment are both close at hand. Because it is so easy to join the ranks of couch potatoes, and because I did not want to become the pin-up girl for the organization, I put down my TV remote control, gobbled down the last remnants of buttered microwave popcorn, and dusted off my membership card in a neighboring health club. It was time to convert from couch potato to a Richard Simmons success story.

I was advised that sedentary people should choose an exercise they enjoy, and start out gradually with their daily regime, building up to a more strenuous workout. Since eyebrow tweezing couldn't, by any stretch of the imagination, be considered physical exertion by too many, I bit the bullet and showed up for "beginner's exercise" class at the spa.

It was written up as "gentle, easy work-out for those desiring an introduction into physical fitness." Thinking that there would be me, a few senior citizens, a couple of expectant mothers, and some high ranking officials of the Couch Potato Society, I eagerly anticipated my first class.

I knew I was in trouble when I walked into the large room. I felt like a Cabbage Patch baby in the midst of a group of Malibu Barbies. There I was, in grey sweatpants bearing the number and name of one of my sons' football teams, a baggy sweatshirt that said "Born to Shop," my dingy sneakers, with my Motel 6® towel stuffed in a grocery store plastic bag. My hair was pulled into a scrawny pony tail, secured by a wide red rubber band from a recently purchased bunch of celery. (Hey, don't laugh, it was all I could find.)

There they were, young, lithe, and in shiny tights, matching cut-to-the-waist leotards, leg warmers, and sweat bands strategically placed around their scrunchy curls. I stood in the back row, far from the mirrors, and close to the exit door.

The neck rolls were OK, and the shoulder shrugs were fine, but when everyone sat on the floor, legs apart and outstretched, and bent their heads to the ground, I realized there might be a slight problem. I put my chins on my chest and decided to fake it. The instructor, clad in spandex snake skin printed tights, shouted above the loud music for us to lie on our backs and extend our legs slowly, from an upright position, toward the floor. On the count of eight, just when I was almost there, she yelled "Hold it for the count of 10, a few inches off the floor."

My legs trembled, my abdomen ached, and I was perspiring profusely. By the time she told us to relax, and I thought it was over, she barked, "four more of these, now." She watched me as if I were a prime candidate for C.P.R., and I hoped she had passed the course.

By the time we made it to the "cool down" exercises, I was ready for a nap, heating pad, and 12 aspirin. My trembling legs supported me as I limped down the stairs, and headed for my comfortable car seat.

I wonder if the Couch Potatoes need a president for their club?

August 22, 1989

SIZE SEVEN REMEMBERED

*T*he cover on the package caught my eye right away.

"LOSE WEIGHT EFFORTLESSLY NO DIETS,
PILLS, OR MEETINGS TO ATTEND."

To someone who has spent the greater portion of the last 15 years unsuccessfully fighting the "battle of the bulge," it seemed too good to be true. I snatched the cellophane wrapped parcel from the shelf at the bookstore, charged it on my increasing bank card debt, and prepared to embark on my journey to everlasting slimness.

I had laughed at my friends who used to diet continuously, and stuffed my skinny little size seven frame with all sorts of fattening foods, never gaining one ounce. A salad was not in my daily food plan, and bread and pasta were the staples of my existence. I really worked to reach the one hundred pound mark, and was constantly eating to maintain that prized weight.

"What goes around comes around" certainly held true, for somewhere between where I was and where I now am, there must have been a major memory blackout. I don't seem to recall being anywhere in between Misses Twiggy and Piggy, respectively. The hip bones that used to stick out in my Catalina® swim suits each summer, causing me untold embarrassment, seemed to have disappeared from my torso. Could it be possible that they have dissolved, or perhaps been absorbed by cellulite? Those collar bones that used to prevent me from wearing open collared blouses are also among the missing, and beneath my chins there once was a scrawny neck that cried out for turtlenecks. Back then, I resembled Audrey Hepburn, now I look more like a real turtle.

There have been grapefruit, liquid, powder, and soup diets. I have weighed two ounces of chicken and fish for dinner as carefully as I had weighed my children, and loved them almost as much. I had eaten so many salads, my nose began to twitch, and I could have authored a Cliff notes version of the Scarsdale

Diet. After I counted grams, ounces, carbohydrates, calories, teaspoons, fats, and sugar content, I threw my calculator at the scale and went through a severe pizza withdrawal period.

I held the dubious distinction of being the only "Lifetime" member of a self-help diet club that had never reached "goal" weight, and I had enough diet diaries to repaper our entire house. Surely this wonderful packet of cassette tapes I had purchased would enable me to break out of my cocoon of fat and emerge the slim butterfly I had once been.

The first tape was introduced by a soothing male voice; "This tape contains hidden subliminal messages which will be audible to the subconscious mind. You will hear only the soothing sounds of nature and peaceful settings, and this tape can be played at any time to reinforce the subconscious and thereby enable it to cause you to automatically establish eating and exercise patterns that will result in desired weight loss. The second tape should be used only at bedtime, as it causes a hypnotic effect. Even if the listener falls asleep, the messages will still be received by the subconscious mind."

The sounds of the ocean waves crashing against the shore conjured in my mind an image of a beautiful white sandy beach. I saw the palm trees swaying in the breeze, and then off in the distance, a large building. The mental picture became clearer, and I could see the chili dog stand. This was not the way this was supposed to work. I yanked the tape out and quickly flipped it over to the sounds of a forest. The birds were chirping, the mountain stream was gurgling, and the leaves, crunching, implied little woodland creatures like Bambi and Thumper playing hide and seek.

The sounds of the wooded forest reminded me of the Great Smoky Mountains; I could imagine the Little Pigeon River and the majestic Chimney Tops frosted with snow. I saw the mountains, and the road leading from the park into town. Before I knew it, I was standing in the candy store, knee deep in taffy, attacking a caramel apple.

The bedtime tape was wonderful; I dreamed I was on a cruise ship and I never left the captain's dinner table. I wonder if Liz and Oprah would like to send me their "before" wardrobes?

SELLING MY SOUL
FOR A PAN FRIED PORK CHOP

"Jack Sprat could eat no fat; his wife could eat no lean,
so between them both they licked the platter clean."

In all books of nursery rhymes, we see skinny little Jack seated across the dinner table from his rotund wife. While he's looking very glum, chasing some green vegetable around his plate, she is relishing her pile of fried chicken. Was Jack ahead of his time, or was he trying to get rid of Mrs. Sprat by forcing her to eat all those horrid little fat grams? Did Mrs. Sprat succumb to major coronary artery blockage before she reached the ripe old age of 21, or did she outlive her lean spouse by 20 or more years, drowning her grief in hot buttered biscuits and milk gravy?

Assuming the Sprats were around before the general populous was made aware of the consequences of a fat-rich diet, I feel it's safe to say they lived moderately happily ever after. It is highly likely, however, that they never experienced the divine taste of a leftover meat loaf sandwich, on white bread, with lots of real mayonnaise.

My brother, who is not named Jack, has lost over 20 pounds since Christmas, by eliminating most of the fat from his daily diet. Because he is younger, has less hair than I do, and I'm supposed to behave like an adult, I feel it's not kind to call him bad names. He frequently shows me how many notches he has moved up on his belt, and how baggy his jeans are in the seat. I refrain from hitting him, and wonder if he ever had to lie on the bathroom floor to get his stomach to flatten out enough to get his pants to button at the waist. I also hasten to remind him that his figure was never inflated by pregnancy, and that I'm still struggling to get off those last few stubborn pounds after the birth of my last child. He reminds me that my "baby" will soon be 25 years old.

The old "anything you can do, I can do better" big sister competitiveness gets the best of me, as I attempt to go fat free. The first essential reference I require is a fat gram counter book. It admonishes to eat no more than 30 fat grams per day. There is a chart that I can write down each and every little tasty fat morsel I consume, and add them up at the end of the day. I quickly discover that the chart is too small, and I must;

a.) get a bigger chart, or b.) eat less fatty foods.

In multiple choice questions, I always liked the "a" answer better.

Bacon and sausage for breakfast will have to be a fond memory. Pecan waffles or a cheese omelet? Unless I want to use up all my fat grams for a day and a half on each of them, forget it. Small portions of cereal, skim milk, fruit, and toast without butter will be the first nourishment of the day. Yum, yum. Lunch is ideally a salad without dressing. I never have been able to figure how anybody, but a rabbit, can enjoy munching on plain lettuce. I dream of rich bleu cheese dressing with those wonderful nasty smelling hunks of cheese, and settle for a bottle of fat free, cholesterol free, low sodium, reduced calorie dressing. It also has chunks, but judging from the taste and listed ingredients, I'd have to bet they are compressed sawdust.

Chicken is fine for dinner, just as long as there is no skin on it, and it isn't fried. (Lucky for Private Sanders he got his promotion to Colonel before they skinned and baked all the birds.) To keep from choking on a dry baked potato, I open a small bottle of butter flavored powder and sprinkle it generously on the steaming potato. It clumps in unappetizing little yellow globs and refuses to melt. If I am a very good girl, and eat everything on my dinner plate, I can have a dessert of fresh fruit. I don't think bananas were meant to be eaten without pudding, vanilla wafers, and a nice thick glob of whipped cream. As an alternative, I can have plain sugar free gelatin, which always conjures up memories of hospital meals.

A hamburger and french fries add up to a week's worth of fat content, so in their place I can have a turkey burger and some steamed broccoli. I'd like to see a fast food restaurant hand that out at their drive through window. Potato chips cannot be brought into the house, for they will surely cast a spell on me, march right into my mouth, and proceed directly to my arteries, causing me great taste satisfaction in the process.

I keep reminding myself that I'm going to be thinner and healthier by reducing my fat intake, but I wonder if the devil has ever before resorted to using a breaded, fried pork chop as a source of temptation.

August 6, 1991

MALL WALKER-THESE BOOTS WERE MADE FOR SHOPPING

The heat and wretched humidity made walking outside more than unpleasant. With a work schedule that doesn't allow time for an early morning walk, and a body that rebels at the mere mention of outdoor temperatures above 75 degrees, I joined the ranks of "mall walkers."

We are fortunate to have a brand new, two-level air conditioned shopping mall within a mile of our house. It opens early on the weekends, before the shops unlock their gates, to accommodate the walkers. When we first began to walk, I had a problem with my shoes; the rubber on the toes wanted to stick on the slick marble tiles of the mall's floors. The shoes stayed put, while I attempted to move on, creating a very awkward stumble every other step. It was not very attractive, and tended to slow me down quite a bit. A stop at the shoe repair booth quickly remedied the problem, and 6 dollars poorer, I was at least able to keep from falling on my nose.

Feeling much more secure in my shoes, I briskly turned the first corner of the mall's upper level. I sniffed the unmistakable aroma of fresh baked cookies ... chocolate chip cookies. The closer I got to the cookie stand, the better they smelled, and the harder it was to stay on the walking course. By the second lap, the oatmeal raisins were just coming out of the oven, and my will power faltered. At the temptation point, into the third segment of the walk, I stumbled past the glass display cookie case.

"Shoes acting up again?" my husband asked.

"Maybe the glue is still wet on the soles," I quickly replied, hoping he wouldn't suspect how embarrassing it would be for me to remove my sneaker, smash the cookie case and devour the entire contents.

To save my dignity, and remove the source of temptation, I suggested that we change scenery and walk the remaining laps on the downstairs level. He reluctantly agreed, and as we got off the escalator, I saw rows of "Final Clearance" signs in front of most of the stores. Now instead of a gnawing stomach hungry for cookies, I began to get the terrible urge to lay plastic cards down on cash registers.

I spied a wonderful pair of summer shorts, and I knew they would probably pay me to take them out of the store to make way for winter coats. I'd stop there on the way out. At the next window, there was a pair of sandals that I had liked earlier in the season; they would be dirt cheap by now and perfect for next year. I slowed down to get a closer look at the mark down tag on a pair of polka dot earrings.

"Why are you slowing down? Is it those shoes of yours again?"

"Uh ... yes. Yes, I think I have a rock in my shoe. I'll just sit here on the floor and get it out."

"Where in the world would you pick up a rock in your shoe walking in the mall?"

"Probably brought it from home," I laughed, straining to read the blurred red sticker on the merchandise directly above my head.

By the time we were finishing the last part of our walk, starting to slow our pace a bit, I told him I was going to the ladies' room and would meet him in 15 minutes at the mall entrance.

I moved faster than the Roadrunner through the stores, with the magic word of "charge" ever ready on my lips. I saved one stop for last, and as I approached my husband, with shopping purchases safely bagged, I waved the bag of warm chocolate chip cookies. The mall walk cost $57 dollars, (counting the shoe repair), and enough extra calories to keep us walking, now forevermore outside in the sweltering heat, an extra mile for another two months.

August 3, 1993

DIFFICULT TO FIND, HARDER TO STAY WITH DAILY EXERCISE ROUTINE

In an all out effort to achieve physical fitness, I have diligently started a daily aerobic exercise. Unlike my younger, slimmer days when I chased my herd of "rug rats" around the house, I have succumbed to an (outwardly) calmer, less active lifestyle. No longer do I hit the floor running every morning, and lapse into a semi-comatose state around midnight, after a 28-hour non-stop day of mothering. I crawl reluctantly out of the bed each morning, gently coaxing my body into transporting me around for another day, and often nod off during the early portion of the 10 o'clock news. Because I am older, and constant maternal worry does not burn one single calorie, I am now what Jane Russell terms "a full-figured gal."

Walking was great, for a while, until the extremely hot temperatures discouraged me from venturing outdoors. Temptation was too great to walk inside the shopping mall, and my charge cards needed a well deserved rest, so I got an exercise video. After doing Jane Fonda's warm-up moves for the first and last time, I collapsed, breathlessly, on the floor. I wisely chose not to attempt to "go for the burn" as she easily completed her famed work out.

Seeking another exercise, I quickly eliminated swimming from my choices. About the only water feat I can manage is floating on my back for a very brief period, about 45 seconds, before gravity pulls me downward. The first time I attempted swimming lessons was at the YWCA®. I was a less than enthusiastic teenager, whose admiration of Esther Williams was stronger than my long standing fear of the water. Everything went pretty well, until I walked onto the diving board for my first plunge. I got to the end of the board, looked down into the pool and decided Esther would have to star alone in her next movie. The instructor, noticing my hesitation, nudged me off the board. I still don't know how I made it out of the pool, but I must have broken Olympic records in my haste to leave, and I never went back. So, until they make adult size

95

"swimmees," I am content to stand solid in the shallow end of the pool, with one hand on the ladder.

As an acceptable alternative means of exercise, I decided to dust off the stationary bike that I gave my husband for Christmas a few years ago. Placing it in close proximity with the television set in the recreation room, I reasoned that the distraction of the TV would make the riding time pass much faster. I started slowly, and gradually built up my speed, and felt the perspiration begin to form. I pedaled faster, and the socially acceptable perspiration quickly changed to very unladylike sweat. My damp hair was sticking to my neck, my pulse rate was accelerating, and my calf muscles were locked, as I checked the timer. Only five minutes had elapsed, and the first commercial hadn't even started.

After five more, seemingly endless, minutes of excruciating stress to all my semi-movable body parts, I decided to do the "cool-down" and add a couple of minutes each night, until I could comfortably pedal for 30 minutes.

The following night, I had a meeting, so I skipped riding. Next night, I baby-sat, and told myself I'd get up 15 minutes earlier the following morning to exercise. I overslept 10 minutes, instead, and promised myself that I would get back to the bike that night. An unexpected dinner invitation proved to be far more appealing, however, and the following evening I brought home a stack of uncompleted work from the office.

Each time I tip-toed past the bicycle, it seemed to say, "You're neglecting your promise to me."

Determined to begin anew, I have allotted 30 minutes out of each day for riding the bike. Looking very much like Margaret Hamilton as she, the wicked witch from "Wizard of Oz", rode her bicycle, I pedal furiously, going nowhere. As I recall, she finally melted into oblivion. I wonder how many hours she rode that bike?

DO MIRACLE WEIGHT LOSS LAB RATS EAT FAT FREE CHEESE?

There is good news and bad news in a recent Associated Press story. Good news for mice; bad news for hungry cats. Good news (maybe) for overweight people; bad news for weight loss centers. Dr. Jeffrey Friedman, of the Howard Hughes Medical Institute at Rockefeller University, announced that research in three labs proves that a hormone called leptin forces the body to burn excess fat, while having no apparent effect on lean tissue. Derived from the Greek word meaning thin, leptin is a protein that is normally produced by one of the body's genes. The researchers have found that mice with flawed leptin producing genes are those that become obese.

The experimental mice that were found to be lacking in leptin, "after receiving injections of the hormone, quickly lost fat cells, ate less, spent more time exercising, and generally became healthier." I'd be willing to bet they were able to squeeze into their old mouse holes a lot easier, and steal the cheese bait off a trap much faster too.

Weight loss was very rapid for the lucky little rodents. Within two weeks, they lost all but 9 grams of body fat. The fat mice who didn't get the hormone shots maintained about 38 fat grams. The first question that arises, in my mind, is how do lab mice get overweight? Second question: Where do they find those tiny mouse scales? Do they pass up the fat free cheese in favor of Gouda and Brie? Are they the ones that escape from their cages at midnight and head for the takeout pizza scraps in the trash cans?

I suppose the thin mice exercise more and count fat grains while their obese litter mates lay around in sawdust all day, dreaming of peanut butter sandwiches and caramel popcorn.

I am enthusiastic about this new hormone discovery, but somewhat skeptical about its effectiveness in humans. I don't believe mice go to parties where they are tempted by canapés, mini ham and turkey croissants, or chocolate éclairs. Their birthdays probably aren't highlighted with ice cream and cake, and their idea of a big Christmas feast is to nibble on the corner of a cookie left out for Santa. They don't have fast food drive-in windows to make calories-to-go quick and easy, nor do they salivate over a plate of spaghetti and meatballs. I'd be willing to bet they don't even crave jelly doughnuts, fried pies or barbecue on cornbread. If someone could put me in a cage, feed me only low-cal tidbits, and inject me daily with a fat consuming hormone, I believe they'd get some pretty impressive human results. It would just be my luck to volunteer for the anticipated experimentation on humans, and they would put me in the group that got the placebo. I'd gain weight on a liquid diet while I watched others in the group become slimmer by the hour as they pigged out on country fried steak, mashed potatoes, and biscuits.

Mice don't do aerobics, stair climbing, jogging, walking, running, or exercise videos. They don't go to support groups or eat portion controlled packaged microwave mini meals.

Nobody ever saw a mouse hyperventilate because it had to lose 25 grams before it's class reunion, or agonize over fluid retention two days before a doctor's visit. Mice don't have to punch extra holes in their belts, or squeeze a size "B" derriere into the last remaining runless pair of size "A" panty hose, five minutes before leaving for work. They don't have to shy away from cameras, buy polyester with elastic waistbands, or scurry to the bookstore to buy the paperback edition of the latest "proven" weight loss diet.

I really hope they find that leptin is the long awaited weight loss miracle, and that there are no side effects or long term harmful results on the body. But until that happens, I'll envy those skinny little lab mice, as well as the researchers that made the discovery. I believe they will become extremely "fat," if their experiments prove successful.

CREATIVITY ABOUNDS ... SOMEWHERE

Chapter

April 10, 1988

Not Sew Easy

*I*n a rare fit of creativity, I thought it might be fun to make a skirt for myself. When the children were small, I used to sew a lot for myself and for them, and it was definitely a big savings compared to "ready made" clothes. First things first, I'd select an easy pattern, and then purchase the amount of material necessary to create my spring wardrobe addition.

I looked on the directory of my favorite department store for "piece goods", "sewing notions," "patterns," or "fabrics," Unable to find any listing that would remotely suggest the department I needed, I went to the floor where needlework and fabrics used to occupy a sizeable portion of space. I searched the floor, and found nothing remaining of the original department. In it's place was an aromatic cookie stand that successfully detained my search for a short while. I asked the young lady behind the oatmeal, chocolate, pecan, and raisin temptation station if she knew where I might find patterns and fabrics. One look at her puzzled face convinced me that our conversation was over.

"Excuse me, but could you tell me where they have moved the material and patterns?" I asked one of the older salesladies.

"Honey, we haven't carried fabrics in several years now. You'll have to go to one of the fabric stores now," she replied.

Gosh, I didn't realize it had been that long since I did any sewing. I recalled how I had made all three of the boys vests for Christmas one year. Many painstaking hours went into every stitch of the three identical red garments, and they were each lined with blue and red printed manufactured silk (better known as polyester, at that time). I had covered buttons in the print, attached them with a short length of gold chain to hold the front of the vest neatly closed, and found that I had a lot of the silk like fabric left.

I made my very first necktie for my husband with the remaining yardage, and then fashioned a scarf for myself. We were going to look like the Brady Bunch on Christmas, and I was so proud of my handiwork.

The big day arrived, and I waited until all the other gifts were opened to give them my surprise.

"Look what I made for us to wear today," I said, swinging out our family wardrobe for the day.

"Oh, gross, Mom, do we have to wear those weird looking vests?"

As a dejected look appeared on my face, their father came to the rescue.

"Boys, Mom has worked really long and hard to make these vests for you to wear, and you should thank her and be proud to wear something so special."

"I made you a necktie, to match the linings and buttons on their vests, and look at my scarf. It all matches, see?" I presented him with his gift. Inaudible groans filled the otherwise silent room.

Everyone in our family kept their coat on for the entire Mass that Christmas morning, and somehow they all managed to spill enough breakfast on their clothes to keep them from being wearable the remainder of the day, as we visited family and friends. My husband's tie had a very large, cumbersome knot at the neck, and it hung a bit crooked at the bottom, so I took pity on him and told him he didn't have to wear it again. At least my scarf turned out well, so my efforts weren't totally wasted.

So what if my last, long ago attempts at sewing didn't prove too successful; this time I had only myself to please. I found the fabric store, selected my pattern, and chose my fabric.

The saleslady added my purchases, and I was shocked when they totaled as much as the cost of a "store bought" item, already made. I asked her to re-add my items: She checked them off the cash register tape. "Five dollars for the pattern, sixteen seventy-five for the fabric, two-fifty for the zipper, plus the hem tape and thread — it's correct, madam."

I wonder if I could find that scarf of mine — it just increased in value.

November 28, 1990

CRAFTS' KLUTZ CHALLENGES CHRISTMAS

The good Lord, in His infinite judgement, gave each of us certain talents. To some, he gave the ability to sing, (hopefully better than Roseanne Barr), or to dance in a manner that would make Fred Astaire and Ginger Rogers envious. Other gifted individuals can sit down at a piano, with nary a lesson, and make the ivories resound with melodies that would make Liberace sound like a beginner.

As the Christmas season approaches each year, I am totally intimidated by a growing number of people who have remarkable capabilities. You've all met them, they are your friends, your relatives, and neighbors. These individuals appear normal in every way, but if you look at them closely, you'll see dried glue on their fingers, and burn marks left by their glue guns. They are the ones that make those elaborate Christmas decorations, and act as if it were the most natural thing in the world to whip up a gross of handmade tree ornaments in two hours.

They come to parties in glitzy, sparkly, hand-painted sweatshirts that defy description, and modestly reply, "Oh, this? Gee, it's the easiest thing in the world to make. You just get these cute little pre-made Santa and reindeer at any fabric store, and ... well, buy a shirt and I'll help you do one."

These talented souls haven't the foggiest notion of what it feels like to be the only junior who flunked bound button-holes in high school home ec class. They never experienced the trauma of not reversing a wall to wall bathroom carpeting paper pattern before ruining their newlywed brother's new apartment decor. Christmas centerpieces they make for the bowling league party are clever, and they would most likely never resort to using Reader's Digests folded in the shape of little spray painted trees.

"I got a red sweatshirt. Now when can we get started on it?" I anxiously ask my crafty friend.

"First you wash it, to make sure it's pre-shrunk, then go to the fabric store and pick out a design to iron on the front of the shirt. If you want to, get one for the back also."

Now you must remember that most of these eager beaver creative souls get an early start on their handicrafts. They storm the fabric stores as soon as the first red and green ribbon is displayed, and make a run on anything that vaguely resembles Christmas. This is already December, and after going to 10 different stores in search of a suitable theme for my shirt, I realize there is a problem. Instead of Santa, a snowman, teddy bear, tree, candy cane, reindeer, mice, bunnies, kittens, stockings, puppies, rocking horse, geese, toy trains, or even a tired old elf, which have been bought up since right after Labor Day, I have a choice of a Teenage Mutant Ninja Turtle, or a marked-down turkey.

"There are no Christmas designs left in any of the stores. Now what do we do?"

She assures me that with a little imagination, some lace, ribbon, a few globs of paint, and a few cleverly placed buttons I can design my own creation. To demonstrate, she snips, glues, drizzles some paint, and in a matter of moments, has turned an ordinary tee shirt into a masterpiece. There are little star topped trees, complete with bows, decorations, and lights randomly scattered on the fabric to create a Christmas forest.

I grasp the glue gun in my hand and feel the creative juices starting to surge. Two hours later, I back away from the shirt to examine my work of art. If Santa is on the New Madrid fault when it gives way, the resulting catastrophe would resemble my shirt.

From now on, I'll leave the crafts to those who are qualified to do them well, and I'll just write stories about them.

July 29, 1997

My Role Model?

You've seen her. She is always smiling, every hair in place, looking like she just stepped from a beauty parlor, crisp, serene, and poised in her pristine outfit. She manages to make jeans and cotton shirts look like suburban elegance, and it is inconceivable to think she would ever be seen in a muu muu and flip flops. She is every organized homemaker's source of inspiration and ideas, and every harried one's worst nightmare. Martha Stewart. The name that is synonymous with perfection and resourcefulness.

She doesn't just cook, she "creates" dishes that are picture perfect. The idea of feeding 30 or 40 dinner guests is fun to her, or so she makes it appear. She not only makes her own beeswax candles for the table, she has probably fired and hand painted the china on her own kiln in the barn. Her table linens are likely to be fashioned from hand-loomed fabric she has dyed with extracts from the plants she has grown in her garden, which is fed by her own compost pile, and planted by her own well manicured hands. She will grain feed the pig that she slaughters and butchers, and harvest the wheat that she mills into flour for the bread that will accompany hand-churned butter, in the molded shape of pineapples.

Her dinner guests will not ever experience the exquisite pleasure of dining on grilled burgers served on paper plates, or tempt their palates with chocolate chip cookies, fresh out of the bag onto a melmac plate. I doubt that she would ever serve iced tea in a jelly glass, or feel that buffalo wings and cold beer make a dandy appetizer.

Martha has her own magazine, television show, line of linens, chauffeur, two estates in East Hampton, N.Y., worth over 5 million, a six-acre estate with a 19th century farmhouse and two barns in Connecticut, a condo in Manhattan, six cats, two dogs, and a daughter. As if that were not enough to keep her busy, it has been said that she requires only four hours of sleep a night, and sometimes gardens by flashlight. The woman is a threat to those of us who find it difficult to function on less than 10 hours of sleep nightly, never can even find a flashlight when there's a power outage, and feel overwhelmed in caring for one six-room house in the suburbs, a schefflera on life support, and a 10-foot square garden with four tomato plants.

Can you imagine what it would be like to have her for a neighbor? She would whip up little petit fours and pate' and invite you over for afternoon tea, while you tried to find a creative way to remove bubble gum from the cat's whiskers and wondered if the kids would mind eating pizza for the third night in a row. She would be the one who always came to the pot luck supper with a rack of lamb, or beef Wellington, while the rest of the neighbors wagged over their tuna casseroles and Tex-Mex dips and chips.

Her house would be landscaped to perfection, with manicured lawn and hothouse varieties of blooms thriving in all the right places.

There would not be dead patches of grass, in circular wading pool patterns, in her yard, and the weeds that invaded everyone else's lawns would not even think of growing on hers. By the time you finished your second cup of morning coffee, she would be outside repainting the trim on her windows. When you stroll out to fetch the paper, still wearing a tattered robe and fuzzy green house slippers, she would appear in the driveway. Dressed in crisp white blouse, and starched khakis, she would present you with a plate of homemade warm cinnamon rolls, and a pitcher of freshly squeezed orange juice.

Don't get me wrong, I love and admire Martha, it's just that she is so intimidating. I keep wondering how she manages to do 36 hours of work in every 24 hour day. I remember when Phyllis Diller said she could only bake one cupcake at a time because that's all she could fit in her dirty oven. Now that's a woman I can identify with.

October 29, 2006

SHOWING A LOT OF LOVE WITH A LITTLE YARN

 used to watch my grandmother as she crocheted. Her fingers were never still as she would sit in front of the television set in her sun room, and I was amazed to watch her create baby booties, doilies, tablecloths, afghans, and bedspreads from yarn of various sizes. With four grown married children, nine grandchildren, and countless cousins, nieces, nephews and extended family, there was always a need for one of Grandma's signature items. She even had labels to sew on the completed projects that read, "Made for you especially by Grandma."

I recall the time I asked her to teach me how to crochet like her, and she gave me a large hook and some scraps of yarn, and attempted to show me the basic chain stitch. My hands perspired, and with tongue clenched firmly between my teeth, after a few more practice rounds under her watchful eye, I finally produced a dingy, damp, lopsided strand of something horrible to behold. I could not envision this foundation ever turning into something anyone would want, so I decided to leave the art of crochet to the expert, and just watch her in action with a newfound admiration. She never completed one project that there was not another one ready to start.

When each of us got married, Grandma made us beautiful, intricately woven tablecloths that would rival the most beautiful spider web ever seen. In order that none of us should ever get cold, we got afghans of all colors and patterns. Sometimes, the colors didn't exactly compliment each other, but always the thrifty survivor of the Depression years, Grandma was determined not to waste anything. Whenever she came to visit, we would take from the back of the linen closet the "hat" cover she made for an extra roll of toilet paper, and put it out to appease her. The purple and orange one I had for our yellow bathroom was certainly a focal point. She had made it even more festive with the addition of some pink plastic rose buds and lilies of the valley that she had found on sale

107

at the dime store.

As the next generation began to arrive in rapid succession, every great grandchild got their own baby afghan and numerous pairs of baby booties. "If you keep the baby's feet warm, he won't have colic," we were cautioned. So we dutifully kept those little tootsies covered, and swaddled them even in the warmest weather, lest they catch cold. Surprisingly enough, none of my children ever had colic. She showed us how to wash everything in mild detergent, and stretch them to dry, admonishing us to never put them in the clothes dryer. She had huge drying racks in her cellar that Grandpa had made for her from lumber and nails, but I had to settle for my living room floor with sheet covered newspapers.

Trying my best to be creative, I once signed up for crochet lessons at one of the local department stores. I advanced from chain stitch to double crochet and was terribly proud to show my grandmother the beginner book of patterns, and let her help me select one for my first project. It was then that I made a shocking discovery. My grandmother, the creator of thousands of handmade crocheted items, could not read directions. Everything she had ever made, she either designed her own pattern, or learned it from watching someone else. We looked through the book together and found something that we both liked. In my best newly developed skill, I read the direction for each row, and began to put together the foundation of my first afghan, as Grandma intently watched.

One month later, I brought my half completed afghan to show my grandmother how well I was coming along. She got up from her chair, walked back to her bedroom, and returned with three tissue paper wrapped packages, tied in her never ending supply of string. While I had been laboring over my first creation, Grandma had completed three of them, with a fourth one well under construction.

I treasure every item she ever crocheted, except for perhaps that toilet paper "hat." I still struggle with directions, and rip out my mistakes more times than I care to admit, but I will encourage and show my own grandchildren how to create from a little yarn and a lot of love, something to warm bodies and hearts for years to come.

No Brainer

The human brain is a complex and amazing organ. In most people, either the right or left side of the brain is dominant, but some seem to have an equal amount from each sphere and can be both analytical and creative. The general consensus is that right brained people are creative and spontaneous, while their left brained counterparts are analytical and logical in their thoughts and actions. It would be wonderful if we all could have a little bit of both traits, but try as we might, some of us just simply cannot overcome that right or left brain dominance in our personalities.

I think I suspected that I was being ruled by the right hemisphere of my brain before I even knew what it meant. While other little girls were playing with dolls and having tea parties, I was writing poetry and dressing up like a cowgirl. I loathed algebra, history and geometry class in high school, but found that the English writing assignments were an absolute delight. Although I leaned toward being very creative, I was a miserable failure in any attempts to put things together. When our Home Economics teacher announced that we were going to make a slip and a dress, I was in a state of utter panic. Why couldn't she just let me observe my more domesticated classmates, and write about what they were doing instead of making me lay out all those confusing paper pattern pieces and figure out how they all went together?

By the hardest, I managed to transform fabric into the required garments, but on the day of the long anticipated fashion show, I prayed that no one would suspect that my tent dress was the easiest pattern I could find, and it was held together with an elastic "cinch" belt, a faulty bobbin stitch and a lot of my own sweat and tears. I was relieved to get a passing grade for the year, but earned the nickname "Twitterbug" from the frustrated teacher due to my inability to sit still in class for the lectures on various fabrics. Fortunately, the slip I made was never seen by another living human being and wound up being used for dust rags at home.

I know women and men that love to decorate their homes and take great delight in searching for just the right paint and fabric combinations to create beautiful rooms. I actually watch the home decorating television channel and marvel at the transformations that decorators can make. I see them take a discarded piece of furniture and with a little imagination, wood glue and paint, turn it into a lovely and useful object. They can combine unlikely colors and textures and end up with a finished product worthy of any magazine cover, but I fail to share their abilities and vision. When I see a wicker top to a clothes hamper, it would never occur to me to transform it into a bedroom wall mirror.

Recently, I got an answer to a prayer when I had to select fabric to re-upholster some chairs. On my first attempt, I cried all the way home, lamenting the fact that I was overwhelmed by all the aisles of different colors and designs and could not make a choice. However, on my second excursion, I encountered an angel who enabled me to make my selections, and not experience another melt down in the process.

When I asked for assistance in finding a particular swatch of material at the desk of a local fabric store, fate intervened in my favor. I explained that, given the choice of the pains of childbirth, a root canal or shopping for fabric, I would gladly choose either of the first two ordeals. The saleslady told me she hated shopping for shoes, and I immediately knew that this was going to be a match made in heaven. I gladly promised to accompany her to purchase as many pairs of shoes as she might ever want if she would help me in my fabric selections. It was a win-win situation for both of us.

Less than an hour later, I emerged triumphantly from the store, yardage securely wound in place around cardboard cylinders and two sample swatches grasped in my sweaty hand to whip out at a moment's notice at cocktail parties, chance encounters in the grocery, or matching it up with paint charts, which ranks right behind same day surgery for me.

November 27, 1989

From Chaos=More Chaos

"Organization is being able to find what you are looking for getting things done, being in control of your life."

The opening paragraph from my latest self-help book seemed to oversimplify the curse of the millions, like myself, who have to face the fact that they are basically disorganized and struggle to focus on overcoming the problem. I once read that one of the best ways to become organized is to make a list every day of all the things, a.) that need to be done, b.) that should be done, and c.) that you'll do if you complete lists a and b.

The first few weeks I labored over my lists, carefully jotting down each task, errand, and appointment on sheets of notebook paper. My mother commented that she could do half the chores on the list in the length of time it took me to write it all down, but I was determined to persevere. Before the end of the first week, I found that I was losing the lists, and not remembering what was on list "A" as opposed to list "C." I reverted to my disorganized manner of doing parts of several tasks, never completing anything.

I decided to get three small notebooks, a purse, a wall calendar, and some post-it notes to stick up in conspicuous places. I had a wonderful time writing in the notebooks, highlighting dates on the calendars, and leaving memos to me, from me, all over the house.

"Mom, why is there a yellow note stuck to the dog's mouth that says 'feed me'?"

"It's part of my new effort to get organized, don't you think I'm getting more efficient?" I responded.

"I guess that's why there are more yellow notes on the plants saying 'I need a drink,' and the bathroom mirror has one of your memos to 'brush, rinse, THEN floss.'"

I ignored the cynical remark, tucked my large notebooks under my arm, and set about my listed tasks. On list "A" I crossed off a load of wash, the breakfast dishes, and prepared to address two birthday cards to mail on the trip to the post office, dry cleaners, and grocery. As I started for the door, I searched in my purse for the car keys. They were not in their recently assigned position within the confines of the large shoulder bag, so I emptied the contents onto the kitchen table in hopes of finding them.

My makeup kit was a hopeless jumble of lipsticks, blusher, mascara, a broken compact, ticket stubs from last month's movie, two grocery cash register tapes, half an emery board, six toothpicks, three sugar substitute packets, and an expired coupon for bathroom tissue. Better clean this out while I've got it here, I reasoned. After removing all the contents of the small bag, I threw away (hooray for me!) the cash register tapes, coupon, ticket stubs, and three of the toothpicks, and replaced everything else.

Still searching for the keys, I was interrupted by answering the telephone. An hour later, caught up on all the latest news from a friend, I began to look for the keys once more. I remembered wearing a jacket the last time I was in the car, and decided that perhaps I had stuck the keys in a pocket. Two hours later, after rearranging the hall closet, I decided to take a lunch break, and opened the refrigerator. Realizing instantly that there were lots of unrecognizable little bowls of fuzzy green things taking root in there, I tackled the job of evicting them from the premises.

1 looked at the clock. It was time to run the car pool, and my list "A" was not nearly one-fourth completed. Finding the car keys in the front door where I had left them the night before, I made a mad dash for the school, leaving behind my notebooks with all the afternoon memos. Glancing at the dashboard of the car as the engine sputtered, I tore off the yellow note inscribed "Gas" and vowed to read chapter two of "Organize Yourself" — if only I could remember where I put it.

October 29, 1991

DODGING THE FURNITURE TAG POLICE

I remember sitting on my aunt's front porch, one humid summer evening, swaying back and forth on the glider. I was fooling with the tag on the vinyl upholstered cushion, and in a moment of madness, I ripped the thing off. Utilizing my recently acquired reading skills, I deciphered the printed warning, "Do not remove this tag under penalty of law".

I felt panic rising in my tightened chest, and envisioned a life behind bars. Had I been old enough for the sacrament of penance, I would have headed for the nearest express confessional line. I carefully looked around, to make sure no one had seen my criminal act, and stuffed the crumpled paper down in the depths of my pocket. I later flushed it to destroy all the evidence against me, just in case they took fingerprints before they put me in the lineup, downtown.

The women in my family had a thing about leaving those tags on furniture. I finally mustered up enough courage to examine another one closely, after I acquired some new furniture of my very own. I didn't dare touch the ones that were attached to all of our "early attic" acquisitions; they came to us with the tags, and I still feared intervention from the law if I tampered with them. How in the world could our children ever understand that Mommy went to prison for taking the tags off great aunt's living room sofa cushions.

The same thing happened with lampshades. We never took that cellophane wrap off the lampshades, and I always wondered why.

One day I got up the courage to ask my grandmother, who was seated on a sheet draped couch.

"Why is that crinkly stuff on all the lampshades, Grandma?

"To keep them clean," was her stern answer.

I followed the examples of my elders, and dutifully stored fancy linens in my "hope chest," and put my good dishes, silver, and crystal in the dining room china cabinet. I had a reserve of gowns that were to be worn, "for the hospital," and knew that linen napkins were only used on holidays and for special guests.

113

These customs were the ones I grew up with, and I felt comfortable with them.

That all changed a few years ago. We had dinner at a neighbor's house. The hostess, my good friend, has a real flair for entertaining. She can make a tuna casserole seem like a gourmet meal, surrounded by candles, table linens, and crystal wine glasses. And she has these incredibly beautiful china plates, with pheasants on them. Every time she puts them out, I can't wait to finish my meal to see if the pheasants are upside down, but they never are. I asked her if she was nervous about using the "good" dishes for our dinner.

"Why would I be nervous? They're dishes, silly, and meant to enjoy food on."

She explained that they would never give her or anyone else any pleasure, locked away in a cabinet, gathering dust rather than compliments.

The more I thought about it, the more reasonable it seemed. Why have beautiful things if you didn't ever use them? I remembered all the treasures that my grandmother had stored away in her cedar chest, and she never got around to finding an occasion she deemed special enough to use them. The embroidered pillowcases and monogrammed sheets, the birthday gift dusting powder and colognes that she said were too expensive for everyday use, the unopened stationary boxes, and new nylon stockings.

When I prepared my lunch, at home, the next day I put my peanut butter sandwich on pretty china, and drank diet cola from a crystal glass, instead of a plastic tumbler. (It really did taste better.) With reckless abandon, I ripped the cellophane from all the lampshades in our house, and then grabbed the scissors and headed for those tags that had plagued my nightmares. If they catch me, I'll plead insanity.

WEATHER OR NOT

Chapter

February 19, 1991

FEBRUARY GROUNDHOG HAS NOTHING ON ST. CHRISTOPHER

The groundhog had lost it. There was no way we were in for six more weeks of winter, so he must need glasses to eliminate the shadows he was seeing. The trees were budding, and the buttercups were peeking from beneath their underground winter hiding places. The temperature was nearing 70 degrees, and it was a beautiful day to indulge the senses in the promise of springtime. The warmth of the day, combined with nature's tangible growth, seemed to dispute the February date shown on the calendar. I threw on a sweater and took off for an enjoyable, although unseasonable outdoor walk.

Expecting to hear a forecast that evening for more of the same type of weather, I was astonished to hear the forecaster predicting hard freeze warnings, and wind chill factors below zero. Must have the wrong channel, I reasoned, and this forecast is for Alaska, not Middle Tennessee. After checking all the local television stations, I felt I owed the groundhog a letter of apology, as I unpacked the winter gloves, scarfs, and long underwear that were headed for the attic.

The moisture from the preceding day's car wash had created an ice cover over my car the next morning. The doors were frozen shut, and the trunk was encased in at least an inch of solid ice. After finally struggling with the front passenger door, I managed to break the ice enough to get the door open and crawled across to the driver's seat. The engine needed to warm up for at least an hour, but frostbite was attacking my nose and eyes, so I chugged away after a long, cold 10 minutes.

The wind whipped at my exposed face as I got out of the car, and I wrapped the scarf tighter around my head to try to ward off the bitter cold air. Was it only the day before that I had worn cotton jogging pants, a short sleeve shirt, and a sun visor? Now I was layered with enough long underwear, turtleneck shirts, socks, and sweaters to rival the Pillsbury Dough Boy. It was as if I had traveled from one area of the country to another in a 24 hour period, and

117

crossed the equator in the process.

The cold snap had definitely gotten my attention, and as I resigned myself to the fact that winter weather was here a while longer, I had to deal with another harsh reality — snow. I don't do well in the snow, unless I can travel by sled, and even that is a bit risky. I get extremely tense sitting behind the wheel of a very large automobile that suddenly takes on a will of its own.

As I watched the snow cover the brave, misguided little buttercup greenery, I dreaded the drive into work the following morning. There would be sliding, stalling, running off the road, and dodging other cars; all of this occurring before I got out of the driveway. I retained in my head the info from the drivers' ed manual; don't use the brakes quickly, turn in the direction of my sliding, and put the car in a lower gear going down a hill. My head remembered all these things, but somehow, it never relayed the messages to my arm and leg reflexes when the time arose.

Having me in control of a car on a snow or ice covered road would be like the wildest ride at Disneyworld. It is a frightening combination of Mr. Toad's Wild Ride, The Haunted Mansion, Space Mountain, and Bumper Cars. The last time I drove anywhere in the snow, I promised St. Christopher if we got back home safely, I'd park the car, and rely on a bus. He kept his end of the bargain, and although I was trying to avoid the two-mile walk to the nearest bus stop, I knew it was the lesser of two evils.

My dear husband, bless him, knowing what a menace I am on snow covered terrain, suggested that he drive me to work. (He mentioned something about having an apparition of St. Christopher waiting for a bus). Before he could finish the words, I jumped into my boots and was out the front door, headed for the passenger seat of the car. He gave me a very curious look when I asked him to run over any groundhogs who might be looking for their shadows.

September 12, 1990

WHEN THE POWER GOES OUT,
START COUNTING POLAR BEARS

Following a clap of thunder, and a flash of lightening, all the lights in the house were eclipsed, and the television fell mute. Nothing to get excited about, I reasoned, all the power will probably come back on in just a few minutes. It was dusk, and if I sat on the screened back porch, the faint remaining light of day was enough to illuminate the pages of the evening paper. By the time I finished working the word jumble, surely the power would be back on, I assured myself.

Soon it became more difficult to read, due to the fast fading daylight, and the intensity of the rain downpour. The growling sounds from my stomach reminded me that dinner was past due, so I went into the silent, now dark, stuffy hot kitchen, The thawed hamburger required immediate cooking, and I relied on the outdoor gas grill, with a little assistance from a flashlight and an umbrella, My husband was out of town on business, so I gathered bits and pieces of leftovers from the refrigerator, and felt quite pleased with my resourcefulness.

After dinner by candlelight, I considered my choices for the remainder of the evening. Rather than telling myself ghost stories, the first priority was to contact the electric company and notify the repair service of the power failure. My neighbors' homes were also in the dark, so I had erroneously assumed that someone had already reported the problem, Thirty minutes of busy signals later, I finally got the line.

"We are currently receiving more calls than we can handle efficiently, please continue to hold the line, and your call will be answered by the next available customer representative," the computerized announcement told me

Because my television, radio, and spouse were all absent, and I was lonely for the sound of another voice, I did as I was instructed by the mechanical announcement. I listened to canned music, which really was a welcome relief from the total silence in the house, and I learned how to count kilowatts as I

119

continued to hold the phone. This was certainly shaping up to be a most unique evening at home.

"How long can we expect to be without power," I asked the long-awaited customer rep.

"We have emergency work crews working in your area, and power will be restored as soon as possible," was the carefully rehearsed response. At least the computer gave me a little cheerful music with its message.

Without the benefit of air conditioning, and the rain blowing in any window I tried to open, the house took on the feel of a candle lit sauna. Time to remember the old adage, "when the going gets tough, the tough get going," and draw on my pioneer instincts for primitive survival.

If Abe Lincoln could read by the light of a candle, so could I.

I rummaged around and found some more candles, and with the illumination from the array of Christmas, Halloween, citronella, and my cherished blessed tapers, quickly scanned the pages of an intriguing book. Maybe Abe was younger when he did this, or maybe he had a better source of reading glasses than the local corner drugstore, but it didn't take very long to figure out these conditions were less than favorable for doing a book report.

Take a hot bath, and turn in early, that's what I'd do. Traipsing down the hall with my assortment of rapidly dwindling candles, I fumbled for my nightgown in the dark bedroom closet, and prepared for a long, leisurely soak in the tub. When the bottom of the tub was barely covered, the water grew cold. Remember, dummy, no electricity means no hot water, either. By this time the bedroom was unbearable from the lack of cool air. I switched on the overhead ceiling fan, and surprise — nothing happened. I made a makeshift fan of newspaper and meditated on being a penguin.

In the wee hours of the morning, I was awakened from my light sleep by the television, clock radio, ceiling fan, every light in the house, and a phone call from the utility company.

"Is your electricity restored, madam?" the cheerful caller inquired.

"I'm sorry but I'm presently counting more polar bears than I can possibly manage. I'll get to your inquiry just as soon as I stop sweating."

July 12, 1,990

DROUGHT ON THE LAND

he heat was unbearable. There had been no rain for weeks, and the ground was parched. Flowers readily drank up the light sprinkling from the garden hose each evening, but their roots were in desperate need of a good soaking, steady downpour of rain. The tomato plants I had coddled were droopy, tall vines with their sparse anticipated harvest struggling to survive. The loud drone of neighborhood homes' air conditioners was constant, and lawn sprinklers danced across almost every dry, brittle yard from late afternoons until sundown.

On my car, there was two inches of dust, and as I approached the car wash, I should have suspected the weather forecast had been revised from, "hot, dry, heat index in the 100s," to something wetter. Scattered showers had been in the weatherman's predictions, but they had been so few and far between, they weren't a genuine concern. From a lengthy line of cars, the number steadily dwindled, and I was pleasantly surprised to find myself the only customer.

The attendant asked, "You wanna get your car washed, ma'am?"

Suppressing the urge to tell her that I had really only stopped to admire their towel collection, I gave her an affirmative nod of my head.

"You want the Standard, Semi-Super, Ultra-Special, Magna Deluxe, or the Supreme Odyssey Illusion?" she asked.

Feeling more like I was choosing from the menu at an ice cream parlor, I asked her to explain the differences.

She snapped her gum, rolled her eyes, and began; "Standard, you get the hood and trunk washed, the rest of it hosed down, and two squares of paper towels to dry it off yourself, and it's $4.75. Semi-Super, the whole car gets soaped and rinsed, your tires are washed with a brush, and the ashtray gets emptied, while a hair dryer is aimed at the wettest spots. That's $6.50. Ultra-Special, you get the outside washed real good, the inside wisk broomed, the rear view mirror cleaned, the bumpers spit shined and they ride it between those big box fans to dry. It goes for $8.95. Now the Magna Deluxe gives you the same as the Ultra Special, except they vacuum the floor mats, spray some air freshener on the inside, and dry it with the hot air blowers, It usually costs $12.79, but today we got a special, and you can get it for $11.98, with a free auto litter bag and a scented cardboard pine cone thrown in."

"What was that 'Odyssey' thing you mentioned, and how much is it?" I wearily asked her.

"Honey, it is really something else, I mean, they do the whole works, put Armor All® on the dashboard, steering wheel, roof, and anything else that ain't metal. They wash all the windows, inside and out, shampoo the floor mats, and de-fuzz the upholstery with one of them little shavers. They run it through the hot wax machine, and shine all the chrome with toilet paper. When it's all done they either spray it with one of our deluxe aroma fresheners — Cinnamon Orange Pecan Coffee Cake, Morning Fresh Sunshine, Ocean Mist, Lemon Pina Colada Divine, Caramel Taffy Apple Cherry Pie, or they stick one of our new air clarifier magnets on the dash. We only have one, it's called 'President's Temptation,' and it's a plastic broccoli stalk that smells just exactly like peppermint — cutest thing you ever did see, and so real looking you'd swear it was the real thing. That's the Supreme Odyssey Illusion, and we take Master Charge, Visa, American Express, and personal checks — it's $27.49, but you get two coupons for a dollar off on the next visits."

I chose the $8.95 option, and proceeded to the cashier's desk to write my check. I purchased two birthday cards, a pack of gum, a soft drink, bag of popcorn, a license plate holder, tissue dispenser, and a new pair of earrings before I exited to my newly cleaned car. Talk about your "one-stop shopping."

Three blocks away from the car wash, the storm clouds gathered directly over me. By the time I arrived home, there was a steady downpour of rain and my unsoiled car had accomplished what no rain dancer, cloud seeding, or learned scientist had been able to do.

September 9, 1992

HURRICANES:
BEING THERE IS NOT HALF THE FUN

The odds of vacationing in the state of Florida during the recent devastation from Andrew are staggering, but there we were, smack in the midst of a hurricane watch. To native Floridians, the threat of impending hurricanes is as much a part of their existence as earthquakes are to Californians. (Both of which are valid reasons for me to continue living in Tennessee.)

Tornado alerts have always terrified me, and as soon as the first high pitched "beep, beep, beep" warning flashes across our television screen, I head for the basement with my blessed candles, a glass of wine, and a large bag of potato chips.

While visiting our youngest son near Tampa, I noticed my husband watching the weather channel with more that his usual interest. Instead of merely getting regular hourly updates on the weather conditions all across the United States, he was fascinated by a large colored circle located in the Southern part of the Atlantic Ocean.

"What is that weird looking thing on the radar screen?" I asked.

Before he answered, there was an update advising listeners that hurricane Andrew had hit the Bahamas and was moving rapidly toward the southern coast of Florida. It was termed the "hurricane of our nightmares," and had 145 mph winds and 20 foot seas, the biggest to hit Florida since 1935, and destined to become the most expensive natural disaster in American history. I recalled one "lasting result" from the great blackout in New York City several years ago, and strongly suspect lots of little "Andrews" and "Andreas" to be born in South Florida nine months after it passes.

"Florida's panhandle counties and the other Gulf Coast states have already begun reviewing evacuation plans," the commentator announced. The huge menacing circle was gaining force as it moved toward land.

"That's us," I muttered. "Evacuation? Is this for real? Will we have to go to a shelter or someplace safe until this thing is over?"

"Nah, Mom, don't get all worked up over this. It's just a bad storm, we'll be OK right here."

"I think I'd like to stay in a church with a priest who gives general absolution," I insisted.

I awoke several times during the night and checked on my bottled water, safely stashed in the refrigerator, and made sure there was enough room for three adults in the bedroom walk-in closet. I grabbed the Sunday morning paper as soon as it was delivered and read that nervous shoppers were stocking up on gas, bottled water, canned goods, lumber, candles, and batteries. In the paper were a list of supplies for the shelter, survival kit checklist, and evacuation routes, zones and shelter listings. I figured out what to pack, secure, abandon, and where to go, and attempted to share the information with husband and son, who were now watching the weather channel together. They cast uninterested glances at me and ignored my panic.

"Mom, chill out, we aren't under a warning anymore. The hurricane won't come this way now, it's changed course." My relief was short lived. I sat down on the couch and watched horrible television scenes of devastation and destruction in Homestead and Miami. It looked like the aftermath of a major bombing. There were houses totally destroyed, their owners wandering the areas, dazed. There was no electricity, water, or phone service. People were virtually cut off from all necessities. In the oppressive 90-degree plus heat there was no shade protection from the uprooted palm trees, no refrigeration, lights, air conditioners, or fans. Where furnished homes had been were now piles of splintered lumber, shattered glass, dreams, and monumental debris.

If storm victims had sought the safety of the shelters, they returned home to find what had been spared of their personal belongings either stolen by looters or rendered unsalvageable by the fury of the mighty storm. They became the target for opportunists who gouged them for $5 blocks of ice and $500 chain saws.

This was the hurricane that will never be forgotten by the ravaged residents of South Florida, who continue to keep their eyes on the sky and their ears open for any new hurricane threats.

January 4, 1994

SNOW PANIC ATTACK LEADS
TO WAR OVER LAST FROZEN PIZZA

*I*t floated to the ground quietly, but before it could land, it was seen by several people, who ran, shrieking loudly,
"IT'S SNOWING!!"

The "Nashville Snow Panic Attack" was quickly full blown. Before the snow flurries were easily visible, the salt trucks were revving up their engines, grocery stores were pulling every item from the store room onto the shelves, and the TV weathermen were basking in their moments of glory. The bulletins continued beeping across the television screen all afternoon, and the radar weather reports outrated O.J.'s trial updates, as the Snowbird turned cartwheels over all the outlying counties around Nashville.

Schools started to dismiss students and sent parents into a frenzy. The hardware stores put sleds, snow shovels, kerosene heaters, flashlights, batteries, and rock salt in plain sight of nervous shoppers. There was a run on firewood, and gas station service bays were packed with drivers in desperate search of snow tires and anti freeze. The entire population of reasonably intelligent, and otherwise rational citizens, was gripped by apprehension and fear.

How silly, I thought. Why in the world does everyone seem to go crazy when a little snow starts to fall? After all just how big a problem could it be to drive home, build a roaring fire, snuggle down with a good book and a cup of hot chocolate, and enjoy the sight of winter's first snowfall?

As I left work, I immediately sensed that there might be a slight delay of four or five hours getting to the interstate. Maybe it was the mile long, bumper to bumper string of cars lined up that tipped me off, but I quickly determined that I'd best be looking for a shortcut. Every street was lined with cars, and nobody was going anywhere. I chose the shortest traffic jam, and felt a slight twinge of fear as the small harmless snowflakes began to grow larger, and fall in bigger bunches.

Half way home, I remembered we were out of milk, and the gas gauge on the car indicated a nearly empty fuel tank. The service station was a disaster, and the little bit of remaining gas I had was almost gone by the time I was able to pull up to the first available gas pump. I watched as people begged, in vain, for the frazzled attendants to produce more de-icer.

The parking lot at the grocery was filled to capacity, and after driving up and down the lanes, I followed a lady, several hundred yards, to her parking spot and waited for her to load 14 bags of groceries, a 50-pound bag of dog food, four snow suited children, and herself into her mini van. Just as I was pulling in the coveted space, an angry man in a four wheel drive jeep gave me a wicked stare and raced off with his snow plow poised for action.

The grocery aisles were a disaster. There were no more shopping carts, so I grabbed canned goods, put them in my coat pockets, and sprinted back to the dairy case for milk. Old Mother Hubbard had more in her cupboard than I found. My hot chocolate would have to be tea, and the roaring fire would have to be started with rolled up discarded newspapers from my recycling bin, as there were no more starter logs or kindling. As I stood in the long checkout line, I saw two men try to race each other for the last package of hot dog buns, and three teenagers make a mad dash for the last frozen pizza.

Home at last, I flipped on the evening news, and watched as the local weatherman fought back his tears as he announced, "The sparse accumulation of snow that we had earlier today will melt tomorrow as temperatures climb above the freezing mark."

Cheer up, fella, it's only the first week in January, there's still plenty of time for Nashville to get really snow crazy.

January 18, 1994

I'm Getting Too Old
For Auto Ice Capades

*W*e watched the green blob move closer to the red dot. The weatherman had been predicting snow for several weeks now, without much accuracy, but I knew that this time he was going to be right. Once the radar screen shows the solid colored mass on top of your city, it's there, and too late to prepare for Mother Nature's ice show.

I really believe that the grocery stores start the bad weather rumors, in order to put everyone into a panic and food buying frenzy. Even though I know this in my heart, I still run to the store, along with 10 million other shoppers and load our pantry shelves for the lengthy isolation ahead. We fight over the last remaining loaf of bread, and race our baskets to the dairy case to confiscate a lone carton of milk. The baskets overflow with hot chocolate mix, popcorn, soft drinks, soup fixings, toilet paper, bread, videos, and bird seed, as we await our turn at the incessant cash registers.

The weather channel becomes the most watched station in the house, and the Snowbird report is eagerly awaited by sled-ready school children. Antifreeze is checked, snow tires put on, wood is dried for the fireplace, and ice scrapers are in place on the dashboard of the car. Throughout the night, I peek through the slats of the bathroom mini blinds, in a mixed sense of dread and childlike anticipation.

It starts out as rain, and then as the temperature drops steadily, I hear the unmistakable peppering of sleet hitting the windows. As the noise decreases, I know that the hard sleet pellets have changed to silent, white snowflakes. By daybreak the ground is lightly blanketed in white, and our entire city shuts down. The newscasters are breathless after reading the lengthy list of school and business closings, and the local weathermen smugly hold their heads up high, after their predictions came true. All of the radio and television reporters urge everyone to stay in and off the roads. I have yet to figure out how they make it in to work.

After a day of confinement, television, and reading, life and work must go on. Despite the dire warnings being broadcast, we venture out to the log weighted truck. The doors are frozen shut, and crack ominously as one is finally tugged open. Inside the igloo on wheels, we feel relieved when the engine starts on the first try. I fumble under the seat and retrieve a can of de-icer, and generously spray the windshield. Turning the defroster fan up to high, my husband cautiously shifts into first gear, and we are slowly, but surely, under way.

The ice crunches beneath the weight of the wheels, and the headlights reflect on the shiny ice covered pavement. Salt trucks don't make it to these side streets, and the final residue of ice will take many days to finally disappear. Coasting slowly to the first stop sign, we slide out onto the main highway, and find a thin layer of very slick ice. As we move along at a respectable pace, the oncoming lights of a less cautious driver move quickly upon us. He speeds by, disregarding the ice, the hills, and the other drivers around him. He envisions his four wheel drive vehicle as an armored tank, and charges forward to be the first on the line of attack. After he sped past, and we were rolling along very well, we saw the tail lights of another car in front of us, barely moving. The "I love Lawrence Welk" bumper sticker and the AARP vanity license plate should have been an indication. Five miles per hour. We were following someone going five miles per hour, and didn't want to scare them by whizzing past them at a breakneck speed of 25, but decided to risk it anyway. As we passed, I caught a glimpse of the terrified elderly man, his eyes wide with fright, neck straining forward, his hands grasping the steering wheel with all his might. Poor old fellow, I thought.

Within a few days the weather improved, and most streets were clear. I ventured out on my own, and as I left my street, headed for the main thoroughfare, I felt myself leaning forward, gripping the steering wheel until my hands ached. I glanced down at the barely moving speedometer, and said aloud to myself,

"Well, you poor old thing."

February 15, 1994

I Survived The Ice Storm

A major earthquake rocks Los Angeles. Was Lorena insane when she yielded a knife to her husband, John Bobbett? Clarksville and surrounding areas are stunned and saddened by senseless murders at a Taco Bell. TennCare program is creating much confusion. Nashville is paralyzed by major ice storm.

Wait a minute, "Nashville," is that Nashville, Tennessee, aka "Music City, U.S.A.," "Athens of the South," and home of the Grand Ole Opry? Oh, yes, it is, one and the same. Nashville, that secure little spot on the map that I call home. In the midst of all the controversy surrounding Tonya Harding and Nancy Kerrigan as they headed for Norway, Tennesseans also find themselves earning an unwelcome spot on the national weather storm news.

Winter's wrath caught us off guard. We, who have relatively mild winters, were not prepared for the massive power failures that resulted from the ice. Having watched New Yorkers and Minnesotans brave the nastiness all winter, we felt very snug, warming our non-frostbitten toes beside our seldom used for heat supply Southern fireplaces. The sleet started on Thursday afternoon, and by nightfall everything was encrusted with a thick coat of ice. Power outages quickly began all across the state, and those who were very patient and persistent phoned their utility companies. Thinking that the power would be restored soon, many went to bed under extra blankets, hoping they would awaken to hot coffee, a warm shower, and sufficient light to read the morning paper.

Most got an unpleasant surprise, and not much sleep, as they were awakened throughout the night by the sound of exploding electrical transformers, and ice weighted trees toppling to the ground. By Friday morning, over half a million were literally powerless. We were among the fortunate few who kept ours, and were happy to share our rare good fortune with family members who stayed with us. We welcomed one of our sons, his wife and baby girl. Our daughter-in-law did not welcome the unexpected case of chickenpox that erupted on her body, in the midst of their exodus from their chilly, dark home. It became a time for real togetherness, and because cable television service was incapacitated, there was ample opportunity for conversations, family videos, radio programs, reading, calamine lotion applications, oatmeal baths, and itch suppressant antihistamines.

On Friday, we attempted to get groceries, or already prepared food, as we drove home from work. Nothing was open. When I say "nothing," I exaggerate only slightly. Passing by the blocks of deserted banks, restaurants, drugstores, gas stations, and grocery stores, and wondering if we had stumbled into the "Twilight Zone," we quickly turned into the crowded parking lot of a fast food chicken place. Powered by generator, to-go orders were being taken, with the average wait of one hour. We left, hoping that we could find something else, and were delighted to find a very busy, neighborhood curb market open. Relieved residents were carrying out bags of ice, milk, bread, batteries, soft drinks and anything remotely useful. It seemed as if we were all wandering around in the aftermath of a surprise bomb explosion.

We feasted at home on grilled cheese sandwiches, tomato soup and Girl Scout cookies. There was no place to purchase additional groceries for those with power, while food spoiled in others' inoperable refrigerators. Cold showers, indoor skating rinks, and candlelight became commonplace in too many households, and chain saws, ice chest, and flashlights were more appreciated than candy and flowers for special Valentine giving.

Giant, uprooted trees lay like fallen giants in many yards, and the damage they created was widespread. Inside houses that still were without power, school children rejoiced over their freedom from their classrooms. Nerves wore thin as multi-generation families struggled to coexist, and long standing friendships were put to the test of close quarters, cold pork and beans, and soda cracker dinners. Sponge baths, floor pallets, and kerosene heaters became daily routine for 7,500 unfortunate Tennesseans, as the warming days stretched into a week, and they hopefully waited for their lights to flicker once more.

For those under the age of 43 who will proudly wear tee shirts proclaiming, "I survived the Tennessee Ice Storm of '94," one word of caution. Beware of those "old timers" who remember the blizzard of '51.

June 19, 1996

PRE-AIR CONDITIONING DAYS:
THANK GOD THEY ARE GONE

"Dog days" are the name given to these typically hot, Southern, humid, summer days of late June, July, and August. This term originated in the Mediterranean region, where the hot weather during this period was not only uncomfortable, it was unhealthy. Dogs were thought to have spells of madness, and Sirius, the Dog Star, rose with the sun and supposedly added to its heat.

Crazy, perhaps, but not mad, our two dogs spend most of their "dog day" waking hours laying spread eagle on the cool kitchen floor. Their favorite spot is directly over an air conditioner vent, but I keep spoiling their preferred repose by moving them away to allow the rest of the household to remain comfortable. When they are outside, they exert as little energy as possible, and seek out a spot under a shady tree, moving only long enough to lap up large amounts of water. Care must be taken when opening the back door, as they stampede, panting, into the house each time it is opened.

From our air conditioned house, into an air conditioned car, to an air conditioned office, we dash quickly about every day. Have a bite to eat at an air conditioned restaurant, and watch a movie in an air conditioned theater. Go to Mass in an air conditioned church, and shop for groceries in an air conditioned super market. We can exercise by taking a walk in an air conditioned shopping mall, or get our hair done in an air conditioned hair salon. Electric transformers run non-stop as they struggle to keep up with the demand for monumental power surges, yet everyone still complains about the awful heat.

I cherish the comfort of all this wonderful air conditioning, but could it be that we have cooled our bodies so much, for so long, that we feel the heat even more? Does anyone else remember the summer nights of sleeping in an attic bedroom, comfortable under a blanket, while a huge window fan sucked cooling breezes through the entire house? Screened in porches often became summer sleeping quarters, providing the sounds, sights and smells of the great outdoors without the aggravation of mosquitoes, flies, and other undesirable pests. We had a big patio in the back yard, complete with a brick barbecue pit, where we often had cookouts. I don't recall the heat, but I do remember digging into the icy cold water surrounding a big block of ice, in a galvanized tub, and fishing out tall glass bottles of soft drinks.

When vacation time arrived, we would pack up the car, and wait until the cooling night time to begin our journey. With all the windows rolled down, and our traveling caps and scarves perched snugly on our heads, we drove many times down the familiar two lane stretch of U.S. Highway 41 to Daytona Beach, Florida. Seems strange to me now that in the heat of summer, we headed further south for an even hotter climate, but we certainly were not alone, as the beaches and motels were always crowded.

In those pre-sunscreen days of sun worshiping, I would spend every waking hour on the beach, greased generously with that glorious tanning concoction of iodine and baby oil, baking myself to a deep shade of copper.

Hand held cardboard fans, stapled to wooden sticks, used to flutter non-stop as summer time church goers vainly attempted to cool themselves. Even with electric oscillating fans whirring constantly, fainting was a commonplace Sunday event, as the combination of heat and fasting caused many to topple over in the pews. The priests, in their vestments, and the nuns, in their stiffly starched headgear and heavy long habits, must have been very uncomfortable, but nobody ever "sweated"; they "perspired."

I know the thermometer climbed over 100 degrees many days pre A/C, but we would head for Cascade Plunge swimming pool, or the pool at Centennial Park, and grab a snow cone or a banana popsicle as we really enjoyed the "dog days" of summer. Now that I'm older, and accustomed to air conditioning, I just like to stretch out on the cool kitchen floor, lap up some bottled spring water, and wait for my turn to lay on the vent.

SNOW DAZE

by Mary Margaret Lambert

They're out of school because of snow, and this one mamma's full of woe.

They search for boots, and gloves, and hats. Do they find them all? Well, perhaps,

But more than likely out of 20 pair, no one can find a size they wear.

So with one black boot, and one of red, and well worn cap upon his head,

Out goes one to enjoy the snow, while I still have two more to go.

We find one brown glove and one grey mitten
(By now number one is getting frostbitten)

Out goes two with shouts of glee — now to outfit number three.

"Where's that coat with the furry hood?" "Doesn't fit"; didn't think it would.

So I bundle him up in an old mackinaw that looks like it was worn
by old Grandpa.

They're finally out — what a brief respite as the doorbell rings.
They've had the first fight.

"I don't care if it is your sled, you gotta share like Mama said."

"Shut your mouth, you whiny brat, or I'll make your lip look very fat."

"It's my turn anyway, you went last, it's not my fault you slid so fast."

"Whatsamatter, Mom, why are you so mad? With all this neat show
you should be glad!"

"Is there any hot chocolate or soup for us? Oh, now Mama, please don't cuss."

In they come and begin to strip, while on the carpet they continually drip.

Into the dryer I toss their array. (Lord, please help me through this day.)

They eat their lunch and then decide there's a 'tough, big hill' down which to slide,

So they dress once more, and here's a new wrinkle, guess who says "I gotta tinkle."

Off they went, — what relief I felt! Then I noticed the snow was starting to melt.

Back they came with complaints anew. "The snow's all gone,
now what can we do?"

("I have an idea with lots of charm, why not take mom to the 'old funny farm.' ")

In comes Daddy at 6:15 with a bit of news that's really keen.

"No school tomorrow for you guys again. Where's your mother?
DRINKING GIN!!!!!!?"

HOLIDAY HAPPENINGS

Chapter

December 16, 1987

RESOLUTIONS THAT MATTER

*I*t's over. The Christmas season is history until next December, and as trees are taken down, gifts exchanged and returned, and leftover turkey is the mainstay of many households, people reflect upon the past year. We berate ourselves for our shortcomings, pat ourselves on the back for successes, and take a mental inventory as we begin our New Year's resolutions.

My own resolutions run pretty much the same year after year, and I begin January with every intention of carrying out my commitments. By February, my self-discipline is on the wane, and by March, I can't even remember where I put the resolution list, much less what I wrote on it. I am, unfortunately, a creature of habit, and much of it is bad. From what I have learned over the years, I know I am not alone.

I suppose the number one resolution, at the top of the majority of New Year's lists, is to lose weight. Some have just a couple of pounds they want to shed, but others, like myself, require more drastic losses. After all the rich, calorie laden holiday goodies, the idea of a more bland, lighter cuisine seems rather appealing. It requires a very strong discipline, however, to go from fudge, jam cake, eggnog, and sugar cookies, to club soda, water packed tuna, lettuce, and halves of bananas. (I have yet to figure out what to do with the other half of ripe banana.)

Because of my constant losses to the "battle of the bulge," this year I'm surrendering. No more buying magazines at the supermarket checkout that promise "how to lose 25 pounds by summer and still eat what you love," and no memberships in weight loss clubs. I no longer will fight, the inevitable girth of my figure. I will buy "Big Mama" panty hose without remorse or embarrassment, wear long sleeves in the summer, renounce belts and anything spandex, and drape all the mirrors in our house.

This will be the year of the "inner self" for me – maybe nobody will notice the outside wrappings if I can perfect my plan. The rules I'm following are very simple, and they were sent on a Christmas card many years ago by a friend.

"Mend a quarrel. Seek out a forgotten friend. Dismiss suspicion and replace it with trust. Write a love letter. Share some treasure. Give a soft answer. Encourage youth.

"Manifest you loyalty in word and deed. Keep a promise. Find the time. Forego a grudge.

"Forgive an enemy. Listen. Apologize if you are wrong. Try to understand. Flout envy.

"Examine your demands on others. Think of your neighbor first. Be appreciative. Be kind and gentle.

"Laugh a little. Laugh a little more. Be deserving of the confidence of others.

"Extend your hand to a stranger and the warmth of your heart to a child. Find beauty in all that surrounds you. Speak your love. Speak it again. Speak it still once again."

Very simple, basic rules for living a better life. I hope that I can make them a part of my philosophy, and perhaps, the size of my "packaging" won't matter so much.

February 8, 1988

VALENTINE FOR MY SONS

*I*t was a crudely fashioned, lacy paper heart, generously smeared with a thick layer of white library paste to make it stick to the piece of red construction paper, unevenly folded in half. It had been painstakingly printed, by small fingers holding a fat blue pencil, to read, "I lov Mom" on the front of the homemade card. On the inside, there was a spiritual bouquet, listing five rosaries, five Holy Communions, five Masses, 10 Hail Marys, 10 Our Fathers, 10 Glory Be's, and five Hail Holy Queens, all pre-printed beneath a holy card with a picture of the Sacred Heart. At the bottom of the card, in large lopsided printed letters was the name of my son, surrounded by a large heart with an arrow drawn in the middle of it. It was destined to remain in my keepsake box forever.

He was soon to learn that it's more fun to send Valentine cards to girls than to Mom, and began to grow into a young man. He thought that Moms were supposed to like cooking, cleaning, and driving car pools; Girls liked candy, mushy cards, and chocolate sodas after a movie. Moms got their thrills from sorting dirty clothes, being a den mother, or giving home haircuts with an electric barber clipper set, obtained with her seven books of trading stamps. Girls delighted in painting their fingernails, having slumber parties, and talking for hours on the telephone. Moms had chipped nails, forgot to wear lipstick, and seemed to never sleep.

Girls always smelled of sweet perfume and dusting powder, and had shiny hair, and sweet smiles. They wore pretty clothes, and giggled a lot. Moms seemed to like old, sloppy sweats, had a lot of grey hair, were always in a hurry, and they frowned most of the time. Girls seemed to think that everything boys said was interesting, and funny, and they would never think to tell a guy to wash his face, brush his teeth, or comb his hair. Girls winked at boys, while moms just closed their eyes, sighed, and seemed to pray an awful lot.

Boys always seemed to be too broke to buy fancy, expensive cards, long stemmed roses, or huge boxes of candy for Moms, but somehow their finances seemed to permit the purchase of balloon bouquets, flowers-by-wire to another town, or large stuffed "huggy" animals for girlfriends. ("Mom, can you please cash a check for me, and hold it for a few days, O.K.? This is an emergency.")

On behalf of Moms everywhere, who still have stashed away, whether in their hearts or their panty hose drawer, an old treasured Valentine, I composed the following "Valentine To Sons":

> *When your head hurts, and your nose gets stuffy, I dose out aspirin,*
> *Gatorade and lots of "lovey."*

> *When your bucks are low, and you need some "dough," who gives you a*
> *"loan," with interest rates low?*

> *I cook your food, and wash your clothes; even trim your stinky old toes.*

> *I love you a bunch, and that is why I do these chores, but I sometimes cry.*

> *I don't expect flowers, fancy gifts or pearls, but always remember...*
> *Moms are still girls.*

> *Kisses and hugs won't cost you one dime, and kind words are free,*
> *so if you don't mind,*

> *Treat me like I was young and tender, 'cause inside I am,*
> *and arguments hinder*

> *My weary mind, and worried brain. Thanks for your time, I fondly remain,*

> *Always and ever,*
> *Mom*

March 4, 1992

FAMILY REVIVES OLD TRADITION:
VIVA SAN GIUSEPPE

*E*very calendar is marked with special days. Family birthdays, anniversaries, and appointments dot the pages of the 12 months of the year. On a Catholic calendar, we get the added bonus of feast days of the saints, some of them obscure, others more popular.

March 17th is celebrated by a large number of people who either are, pretend, or want to be Irish. On St. Patrick's Day, green carnations, ties, and ribbons seem to be the uniform of even very un-Irish appearing folk. Parties, music, huge parades, lots of green liquid refreshment and wee merriment abound. Shamrock bedecked greeting cards are exchanged among friends, and 'tis surely a great day for the Irish.

Two days after St. Paddy's day, when some are still feeling the same color as their lapel carnation, there is another popular saint's feast day. The feast of St. Joseph, spouse of Mary, and foster father of Jesus was first commemorated about 1324, on March 19th. The Franciscans were great publicizers, and by 1479, the feast of St. Joseph had spread across Europe. St. Joseph was known for his patience and his unfailing submission to God's will. He accepted his position as husband to the Virgin Mary, worked as a carpenter in Nazareth, and provided the ideal father figure in the early life of Jesus.

In my ancestors' native Italy, St. Joseph's feast day was commemorated by erecting altars, adorning them with pictures and statues of St. Joseph, large bouquets of fresh flowers, and many candles. The litany began nine days prior to San Giuseppe, and was recited every night in anticipation of the feast day. Everyone dressed in their best clothes, and brought their finest baked goods to share. As patron saint of workers, he was revered greatly by the Italian people. In the Litany to St. Joseph, he is invoked as not only the patron of workers, but families, the poor, sick and dying, fathers, priests and religious, and devotion to Mary. He is second in his holiness only to Mary.

When my great-grandparents, James and Katherine, came to America from

Italy, they left some of their traditional celebrations behind. Upon the birth of the youngest of their eight children, they invoked St. Joseph to spare the life of their child. They made a promise to St. Joseph to not only give the surviving baby boy his name, but to honor his feast day every year. They kept their promise, and San Giuseppe became a happy occasion for family members to gather together in prayer, and praise St. Joseph for his intervention and aid. My father, uncles, aunts, and cousins all congregated for the annual celebration, and old photographs reflect the festive gatherings. It is always interesting when prospective suitors of the younger family members are invited to this long standing family celebration. If they stay, we vote them into the family.

Great grandma and great-grandpa's house burned, but the picture of St. Joseph was miraculously unscathed in the devastation of the fire. After their deaths, however, the celebration of San Giuseppe died also. In the early 1950's, one of their grandsons, Tommy, was inspired to revive the San Giuseppe feast day celebration. He and his wife invited family members, and a beautiful altar was adorned with bouquets of early spring buttercups, carnations, and candles. The rosary was sung in Italian, and the litany to St. Joseph was recited by all present. Following the prayers, the youngest family members scrambled on the floor to collect pennies tossed by the adults. Italian sweets and donuts were then shared over family news and amusing stories.

After almost 40 years the San Giuseppe feast continues to be celebrated at Tommy and Nora's home. The ageless picture of St. Joseph still adorns the flower bedecked altar, and the same prayers are offered for deceased and ailing family members, and for the protection of St. Joseph during the coming months. I regret that I don't know enough Italian to do justice to the recitation of the rosary, but I feel the spirit of my ancestors, and I know they surely must smile when they hear all of us shout, in joyful praise, "Viva San Giuseppe!"

March 19, 1988

An Easter Alleluia

"*Here* comes Peter Cottontail, hoppin' down the bunny trail; Hippety, hoppity, Easter's on its way." Time to get out the patent leather pumps, straw hats, short sleeve shirts, white purses, and summer sport coats. Open the windows, go for a walk, make a jar of sun tea, and feel the warmth of spring easing into the senses, once again.

The lure of the beautiful first day of spring enticed me to visit the park. I listened to the melodious sounds of a flute and guitar, played by two young musicians sitting on a quilt. Their beautiful melodies were interrupted occasionally by a blast of soul or rock music coming from the radio of a passing automobile.

The music seemed to drift and mingle with the movements of the spiraling kites that held the attention of several children. They ran, holding the kites in outstretched arms, until the gusty March winds took hold of the paper toys and whisked them heavenward. The bright colors, against a cloudless blue sky background, created a collage of motion.

I watched, as little ones were led to the edge of the lake by parents and grandparents to re-enact an ageless ritual: bags of popcorn, stale bread, crackers, and rolls were tossed into the water, and quickly gobbled up by the noisy ducks. They quacked loudly, in appreciation, as they fought to eat the food, and delighted the children with their antics.

There were people everywhere; students, lovers, walkers, bikers, photographers, poets, babies, teen-agers, senior citizens, nurses, doctors, construction workers, and policemen, all creating a Norman Rockwell painting, come to life.

The birds were chirping, flying to their nests, now visible, but soon to be hidden by the leaves that would burst forth from the swollen buds on the tree limbs. They hopped around on the ground, poking their beaks into the warm, moist earth, in search of food, or bits of twigs and string to complete their lofty perches in the tree boughs.

Gone were the sniffling colds of winter. Vanished were the aches of influenza, the coughs of bronchitis, and the chills from pneumonia. No more driving on snow slickened streets, or getting towed out of ditches.

Trade the snow shovel for a weed eater, the kerosene heater for a fan, the hot chocolate for a cold glass of lemonade, the long red flannel underwear for tennis shorts, and the heavy duty body moisture lotion for sun tan oil. Pack away the stocking caps, mittens, boots, scarves, and wooly socks. Get out the garden tools, the lawn furniture cushions, patio umbrella, and the lawn sprinkler.

"We must live through the dreary winter, if we would value the spring;
And the woods must be cold and silent before the robins sing.
The flowers must be buried in darkness before they can bud and bloom,
And the sweetest, warmest sunshine comes after the storm and gloom."

—*Anonymous*

He is risen! Alleluia!

MOTHERHOOD: NO OWNER'S MANUAL

*J*ust a mother ... that's all some women long to become. Those that are successful are amazed that their offspring ever survive the maternal blunders and mistakes. There has yet to be written a book that will adequately prepare any female for the task of motherhood.

What woman, in her right mind, ever dreams of driving a beat up station wagon, packed with surly children, 1,000 miles in a week's average schedule? If anyone told us that we'd steal pennies from our baby's bank to pay a monthly bridge club ante, we would never have believed it. We play with dolls when we are young, poking pretend food into an ever silent painted mouth, never imagining that real, live breathing dolls are prone to colic, diaper rash, diarrhea, allergies, and teething pain.

Novice moms take lots of pictures; keep the baby book updated daily with baby's first word, car trip, tooth, haircut, step, and successful potty results. They organize the baby food jars, pre-soak the formula stains out of the new soft cotton gowns, sterilize bottles, pacifiers, and the tub toys, and cross stitch a sampler with the vital statistics of their firstborn. They "bond" with the baby, and call the pediatrician hourly the first month of the infant's life.

When subsequent brothers and sisters appear, as they tend to do, Mom eases up a bit.

She realizes she's fighting a losing battle, and might as well compromise a few of her ideals. Baby number two gets a few less slots in the family photo album, has a few missing gaps in the baby book, dines on surprise meals from the unlabeled baby food jars that his older sibling has stripped, and shares his bottle with the dog on occasion. By the time the next babies are born, the baby books hold little more than random notes, "potty trained successfully before first grade," "has not quit talking since age 13 months," "shows great artistic ability with crayons on freshly painted bedroom wall." The photos are scarce, usually amidst a group at Christmas or birthdays, and by now, the pediatrician is consulting with Mom on problem cases.

As children grow from infancy into all the other stages of childhood, mothers must adjust to the changing needs and demands, and some do it much more easily than others. I suppose there are mothers that never lose their cool, and sail through the "wonder years" effortlessly, certain of their abilities and their plan of action. I just don't happen to know any of these types, thank goodness. We struggle with orthodontists, orthopedists, "mean" teachers, "unfair" coaches, and broken bones, friendships, and romances.

When puberty arrives, it is a very tempting time for Mom to leave home. She checks the scalp of her sleeping adolescent for the sign of the devil, and wonders if either of them will survive these difficult years.

While the rebellious teen fails to see beyond the pimples and the unreasonable rules of the parents, the mother has to constantly reassure herself that this ugly duckling of hers will really turn into a swan someday.

There is no owner's manual for motherhood, it is an on-the-job experience. There are no "perks" with the position, and many of us frequently fail to measure up to the task. Mothers are not perfect, not infallible, and all are merely human. They respond well to hugs, kindness, understanding, non-collect telephone calls that don't ask for anything, and sentimental cards on Mother's day.

"God couldn't be everywhere, so He invented mothers," should be revised to "God is needed everywhere, but He's working overtime, always, with mothers."

June 5, 1995

NEVER HAS THERE BEEN A FATHER
AS WONDERFUL

He held his infant son for the first time, looked down at the miniature version of his own nose and chin, and thought, "What a fine boy this is. Never has there been a son as wonderful as mine."

Through the months of infancy, he assumed an active paternal role in the baby's life. He learned to change diapers, make formula, and developed just the right amount of pressure in a back pat to produce a wonderful burp. He could bathe, feed, and amuse his son very well, when the need arose, but had some difficulty in maneuvering small limbs through arm and leg openings in sleepers. It was an awesome feeling to have such a helpless little human so dependent on him. During the day, he would glance at the 5 X 7 framed photo of the baby on his desk, and eagerly scoop him into his arms as soon as he came home from work.

He coaxed his son into taking his first faltering steps, holding his out-stretched strong arms toward the little guy, assuring him that his Daddy would be there to catch him. Before long, the unsteady walk turned into a confident run, and the chubby legs grew longer and slimmer with each passing year. He spied the baby's first tooth, a white bubble under the surface of the bottom gum, took pictures of it when it broke through, and financed the tooth fairy's visit six years later when he had to pull the same tooth to make way for a more permanent resident.

They went to the barber shop together for the toddler's first haircut, where he dried his son's tears, and wiped his runny nose, as the barber transformed a baby into a little boy with a few skilled snips of his shears. He taught him to lace his shoes, button his shirt, memorize the multiplication tables, tie a necktie, shave, bait a hook, skip a stone across a creek, pitch a tent, throw a curve ball, whistle through his teeth, pump gas, and spot a penalty during a football game.

147

He cut up his food, steadied him on a two-wheeler, made him finish his homework, helped him build a winning car for the Cub Scouts Pinewood Derby, and told him stories about his own childhood. He instilled love, faith, honesty, character, loyalty, and a strong sense of responsibility in the boy, not by words, but by his own example.

He sat beside his son in the front passenger seat of the car, reminding him of stop signs, speed limits, and merging traffic, and reluctantly permitted him to drive only to church, school, and to take Mom to the grocery store in the family car. Throughout the defiant and trying years of adolescence, the father remained firm and waited for the boy to mature. He slipped him money on prom night, filmed a video of his graduation, and stood proudly beside him on his wedding day.

***

He worried about his Dad. His appetite wasn't what it used to be. He coaxed him to eat, and enticed him with promises of desserts as he cut up his food for him.

With his reflexes slowing down, and his eyesight diminished, he didn't think his father should still be driving the car, but his mother depended on him to get her to the store, doctor, bank, church, and the beauty shop.

Dad was getting a bit wobbly when he walked, so the son steadied his father with his strong arm as they walked into the barber shop. His father repeated the same story many times, and the son patiently listened, inserting the proper responses whenever the old man paused. He helped his father with the shirt buttons that challenged his arthritic fingers, and pointed out the penalties when they watched football on the big screen TV. The father watches his son with his own children, and feels a deep sense of peace and fulfillment.

As the father dozes, his son looks at the wrinkled face, seeing his own aged reflection, and is amazed how wise his father has become over these past several years. He whispers to himself,

"What a good man he is. Never has there been a father as wonderful as mine."

August 27, 1990

LETTERS HOME:
MIKE STILL PRAYS FOR AMERICA

The yellowed pages of the letter were dated September 17, 1917, and the postmark was Atlanta, Georgia. I read the following excerpts, written in my late grandfather's unpunctuated, scrawled penmanship:

"Well, I will not get to go to Non. Com. school tonight because I had to work in the kitchen today and just got through. Had to cut stove wood mop the dining room and kitchen and wash dishes for 300 men and it certainly was some job. We have to turn out our own washing and you should have seen the washing I turned out Friday after a long hike of 20 miles. We do not do any drilling on Saturday because we have to prepare for inspection. Your uniform has to be clean and your necktie on and all of your clothes clean. I have got blisters all over my feet and they are sore as a boil. I am going to the hospital in the morning with my feet and my arm. We got vaccinated and I sure have got a bad arm. I want to write to everybody but can't do that because I have not got the time. We get up in the morning about 5 o'clock and go to revelee at 5:15 and eat breakfast at 6 o'clock and go out to drill at 7 o'clock. Drill until 11 o'clock and eat dinner such as it is at 12 o'clock. Go back to drill at 1:30 and drill until 3:45 and come in and clean up your barricks and go to supper at 6 o'clock go to Non Com school at 6:30 and get out of there at 7:30. So there is my day taken up and I have not got time to do anything."

A postcard, from the American Red Cross, dated June 3, 1918, and signed by my grandfather, bore this simple form printed message to his parents:

"The ship on which I sailed has arrived safely overseas"

October 9, 1918, Bordeaux, France

"Dear Mother & Father,

Well, today adds one more year to me and I am 24 or 25. I am telling you the truth I have been laughing all day not knowing how old I am. Can you beat that? I sure hope another birthday will not find me over in this country and the way things have been going I do not think I will although you can never tell. I did not think I would ever come over here but 10 days from today I will be over here 6 months and will wear a service stripe but Mother here's hoping that I will not get to put another one on."

Twenty six years later, after Ewing returned home safely from World War I, there was another letter. This one, from his youngest son, dated November 12, 1944. It was headed simply "South Pacific",

"I suppose I have been kinda slow about writing, but please understand that it's not because I haven't been thinking about you, because all of you are in my thoughts constantly. It's just that we've been so darn busy making invasions and stuff that so little of our time can be called our own. I'm truly in the Navy now, because that's about all we have time to consider.

I guess maybe this thing had better end pretty quick, before that niece of mine gets too big to pick up. It's unbelievable, I guess I must be getting old before my time. After all, I will be nineteen in a few more days. My first birthday away from home and the heck of it is, it's my last teen-age one, and here I am in New Guinea, a substitute for hell. Yes, I got a big taste of the Phillipine invasion. We struck on the island of Leyte, which is right in the midst of that God forsaken outpost. We had such a big taste of it that I'll never be able to swallow it all. At any rate, I'll have lots to tell when I come back home. Tell 'Mike' to keep on praying for her Uncle Dink, because maybe her little prayers will keep us as lucky as we've been so far.

Love, As always

'Dinkie'

P.S. If you don't hear from me for sometime, now don't worry, because we'll probably be out settling another score."

My Uncle "Dinkie" made it home safely from World War II, luckier than his older brother, who lost an eye while serving in the Army. My father, who served also in World War II in the Army Air Corps as an airplane mechanic, along with his older brother, an officer in the Air Force, were also gratefully welcomed back by our family. My husband's cousin and one of mine weren't as fortunate, however, and they gave their lives in the service of our country. With loved ones serving in the military in World War I and II, Korea, VietNam and more recently, Afghanistan and the Middle Eastern conflicts, I celebrate the Fourth of July for each of them and the sacrifices they endured for our freedoms in this great country. Although many of them have passed away now, I know they still hear "Mike's little prayers" for the future of the America they so bravely and proudly served. God Bless America!

October 5, 1993

THE CHILDREN MAY BE GROWN, BUT MOM STILL LOVES GOBLINS

"Trick or Treat, smell my feet, give me something good to eat." The sing song chant of Halloweens past comes back to mind as I see the pumpkins replace planters on front porches. Every year, since our own sons are no longer living at home, I still prepare for the deluge of neighborhood children on the night of October 31st, and at bedtime I reluctantly snuff the remains of a candle in the lonely jack-o-lantern. After the first year, when we had only three or four little goblin beggars, I bought only treats that we liked, since we were forced to consume the undistributed remaining goodies. (Forget about those awful orange and black, paper wrapped imitation peanut butter taffy blobs, that always get thrown away just before Thanksgiving.)

With the exception of a few very familiar little ones, under the watchful eye of Mom or Dad, no longer do diminutive ghosts, and witches go from door to door, ringing neighbors' doorbells in search of candy and other snacks. I remember when the streets of our subdivision were full of costumed children, clutching large bags and king sized pillowcases filled with their loot. My innovative friend and neighbor rented a different costume every year, and the children loved to be greeted by Minnie Mouse, a very realistic gorilla, or a convincingly wicked witch, complete with nose wart. There was a steady stream of children and adults passing through our living room and kitchen all evening, munching on popcorn and washing it down with apple cider. The taped sounds of a haunted house and the dim flicker of candles created just the right Halloween atmosphere, and all the dirty clothes stuffed in a pair of blue jeans and a flannel shirt made a convincing dummy, hanging from the maple tree in our front yard. Even the ever present cobwebs in the corners of the living room gave me the reputation of a realistic decorator, rather than a too short, haphazard housekeeper. Our black cat was also a year round resident, but on Halloween, she became a somewhat mystical and foreboding attraction.

All Hallow's Eve, the night preceding the Christian holiday of All Saints, originated as a Celtic festival for the dead. It was believed that on this night witches and warlocks flew abroad, so huge bonfires were built to ward off the unwelcome spirits. If I suspected, for one moment, that I was going to be visited by witches and warlocks, it would take more than a bonfire to make me feel secure. Perhaps a sack of garlic around my neck, and a two pound bag of chocolates on hand, in case they felt a craving, might alleviate some of my anxiety. From costumed saints to present day Ninja Turtles and purple dinosaurs named Barney, children of all ages love pretending to be someone, or something, else, even if just for one night. Not terribly apt at whipping up a wearable ensemble on my sewing machine, I used whatever was available for my childrens' Halloween costumes. There was the robot, created from silver spray painted shoe boxes, pipe cleaners, and various flashlight parts, a pirate wearing my red bandana, hoop earring, cut offs, and a black construction paper eye patch, Pee Wee Herman in a garage sale suit, white shoes, gloves, and slicked down hair, and the very imaginative "unknown grocery bagger" with a brown paper bag over his head.

No longer do many trick-or-treaters knock on doors that may shield them from monsters that don't wear identifying costumes. If a child collects a sack of candy that has to be X-rayed before it can be eaten, who needs it? The safe trend now is for parties, sponsored by churches, private organizations, and shopping malls. Little Mermaids, and Aladdins will don their store bought costumes and masks, and join the homemade ghosts, pirates, mummies, clowns, Draculas and witches for refreshments, prizes and adult supervised entertainment, and behind one of those grown up masks there will be a writer whose favorite holiday is Halloween.

November 17, 1986

LOVE: THE MAIN INGREDIENT

*A*s the last of the autumn hued leaves cling bravely to the near naked tree limbs, and the aroma of wood fires permeate the crisp cool air, the mind and spirit are prepared for an annual fall celebration of Thanksgiving.

College students stuff a semesters' worth of dirty laundry into mammoth bags, lock up their campus residences, and join the majority of America's population in traveling familiar paths that lead, for some, in spirit only, homeward.

Kitchens are in a constant state of use, as preparations are made for the turkey dinner that commemorates the first Thanksgiving of our founding fathers. Recipe books are dusted off, and family favorites are once again sought out, to be painstakingly assembled. It seems to me there will be one dish that will grace almost every table across our great nation. On this fourth Thursday in November, though the ingredients and preparation vary as widely as do the faces of the chefs, no self respecting bird should make its' appearance without its' time honored accompaniment — the dressing.

In our family, as we have a North-South merger, it has always been customary to recreate the Civil War at the dinner table, as we indicate our choice of preferred stuffing. As they are the majority group, the "Yankee" recipe tends to always win out over the "Suthin," (as it is teasingly called by my in-laws). My husband's family has taken a great deal of pride in their concoction, which is baked in the deep abyss of Big Bird. Being an eager newly acquired daughter-inlaw, long years ago, and not wishing to displease my new family members, I dutifully attempted to sample the grey, unappetizing looking mixture.

My taste buds were assaulted by a brand new experience, my stomach rebelled, and I gained immediate disfavor from my new in-laws. Fortunately, over the years, I have been able to restore their favorable judgment of me by assisting in the production of three additional male members to carry on the family name.

We now have two varieties of dressings at our family gatherings, and the second and third generations of this very loving and vocal group are given I.Q. ratings, based on their choice of either the white bread based, Northern rendition, or the cornbread casserole version. The younger family members wisely sample both offerings, as this holiday falls very close to Christmas, and they do not wish to anger any of Santa's helpers.

Each family has its' own favorite recipe for dressing. The ingredients run the gamut from all sorts of breads, spices, meats, and other preferences, some are very ethnic in origin, and require a great deal of preparation. Others, like the rendition I prefer to use, rely on the help of commercially packaged ingredients as a base.

No matter what the finished product, or where it is consumed, there is one main ingredient in each and every bite of dressing. It was generously laced throughout the dressing I most fondly remember, as I hope it was in yours. My mother knew the secret ingredient, and she used it lavishly for as many Thanksgivings as we were blessed to have her with us. It was love. Go ahead and have as many helpings as you need or want.

MY PLASTER JESUS

The weeks preceding the Christmas holiday had finally culminated, and all the brightly colored wrapping paper and carefully chosen matching bows were now crumpled into wads of rubbish. The hours of baking, sewing, shopping, and addressing cards were a thing of the past, until next year, when the entire process would begin once more.

The stockings above the fireplace had been emptied, and were drooping from their hooks, and the once bright, crisp red bow that had adorned the mailbox was now weather-beaten and faded. Surely the tree was ready to come down. It, a lifelike facsimile of its live counterpart, didn't shed it's artificial green needles all over the carpet, but after taking up a large area of space in the family room for most of the month, it was time to dismantle it.

I plugged in the string of small lights surrounding the nativity scene, as if I could prolong the inevitable end to this joyous season, and I looked at the tiny figures once more before I packed them away in the attic for another year. These ceramic figures had once belonged to my grandmother, and had been made for her by my cousin. Grandma had cherished her miniature likenesses of Mary, Joseph, the Kings, shepherds, animals, angels, and the Holy Babe, and she had told me on her final Christmas that she wanted me to take good care of her nativity set.

Although the first Christmas without Grandma was indeed a sad one, I had felt somewhat closer to her when I looked at her familiar handwriting on the outside of a string-secured box, which was labeled: "Nativity Set. Fragile." I had carefully unwrapped each statue and set in it its proper place either inside, or near, the wooden stable. The shepherd was there, complete with a few of his friends and a flock of sheep. The three kings were all intact, along with their majestic camels, and the donkey and cow were placed near the spot reserved for the figure of the Baby Jesus.

I had searched, in vain, for the small statue of the Christ child, going through each piece of protective wrapping paper carefully. It was a mystery. I knew that the statue had been there the preceding year, and knowing how meticulous Grandma was, I refused to accept the idea that she had neglected to put this most important part of the set in it's proper storage spot. For four years, I attempted to replace the missing figure, without success. Everywhere I went, I looked for a Baby Jesus that would fit in with the rest of my statues. They were either too big, not the right kind of ceramic glazes, or could not be purchased separately. When people asked where the Baby Jesus was, I would tell them that He was coming soon, but I didn't know how long it would take to get him here.

A lifelong friend heard of my plight, and being very involved in ceramics, she made me an exact duplicate of the original figure for my birthday gift two years ago. At long last, the nativity set was restored to its original entirety. The first year I eagerly placed the tiny coveted statue in the center of the stable, I realized that Grandma was still teaching me a lesson.

It didn't matter what the time of year, the Christ child was always there, whether seen or unseen. He wasn't packed away every year at the end of December, amidst tissue paper in a box in the attic. Grandma kept Him with her all year, in a very special place that was always with her at all times, and she wanted me to do the same. He lived in her heart.

LOVE AND MARRIAGE

Chapter

9

October 17, 1989

BETWEEN SCARLETT AND RHETT,
LUCY AND RICKY

"The joys and sorrows are now hidden from your eyes." The priest spoke the words, but they were just part of the marriage ceremony that united two very young people, and the meaning was too remote for us to fully comprehend at the time.

Our late fall wedding was the culmination of months of planning and eager anticipation. My mother encouraged us to have a big wedding, perhaps to compensate for the one she and my Dad had been unable to have, and since all we cared about was getting married and living happily ever after, we willingly went along with any suggestions she had. I hogtied my prospective bridegroom and we selected china, silver, and crystal patterns for formal and everyday use. It was extremely difficult to convince him that we needed anything other than melmac dishes, and aluminum tumblers.

The morning of the wedding finally arrived, and despite butterflies and teary uncertainties, I wobbled on shaky legs down the center aisle of the Cathedral, clinging to my father's arm. Looking toward the front of the church, I focused on the handsome face of my intended spouse, and all the butterflies settled down.

We didn't realize how young we were, or what we were going to confront in the upcoming years. Perhaps if we had, it would have been too frightening, and we would have lacked the courage to meet life's challenges. If we had understood what was ahead of us, would we have exchanged wedding bands and made a lifetime commitment?

He suffered through burnt toast, undercooked chicken, lumpy mashed potatoes, tough chuck roast, and lots of variations of hamburger and tuna. The pretty everyday dishes were saved for company, we acquired a set of melmac, and some aluminum tumblers, and stored the silver and china away in Momma's attic. I learned to stretch a paycheck, iron a dress shirt, and darn a sock (verbally as well). Both of us worked every day, and our night out was usually spent at the grocery or the laundromat. We looked forward to Sunday dinner at his folks' house, and managed to visit my parents, at supper time, once every week. I don't know which of us was the happiest about not eating at our apartment; me, not having to cook it, or him, not having to eat my mishaps.

As my waist began to disappear forever, we anticipated the two of us becoming three. He didn't know he'd have to endure my morning sickness, cut my toenails when they were out of my reach, or massage the leg cramps that woke us both in the middle of the night. We weren't prepared for the complications that caused us to lose that first baby boy, nor the following miscarriages, but neither were we ready for the overwhelming joy that accompanied the successful birth of each of our three robust sons.

We learned about pediatricians, emergency rooms, bicycle parts, Christmas lists, puppies, kittens, turtles, football, basketball, baseball, Cub Scouts, and the tooth fairy. We conquered homework, housework, yard work, and no work. We've survived moving days, job crises, health traumas, births, deaths, romances, acne, and puberty. We've balanced check books, hectic schedules, parental discipline, and meals. There have been broken bones, broken dishes, broken hearts, broken curfews, and broken rules, some mended with glue, others with love and reinforcement. We have camped, in a wet tent, in the mountains, survived a cross country family vacation in a van, and marveled at the beauty that surrounds us in many areas of God's world.

I have watched football when I should have been vacuuming, and he has danced with me when he would have preferred being a couch potato. I have seen him unshaven, unhappy, and unsure; He has seen me weep, listened to me complain, and watched me age. There have been times, I'm sure he would have liked to send me to Siberia — one way, and I've had moments when I would have willingly gone.

Somewhere between Romeo and Juliet, Scarlett and Rhett, Lucy and Ricky, and Miss Piggy and Kermit are we as we celebrate our 30th wedding anniversary. We have laughed a lot, cried a little, and embraced our crazy, wonderful life together.

"For richer, for poorer, for better, for worse, in sickness and in health."

May 23, 1988

WEDDING BELLS ARE RINGING

*J*une being the traditional wedding month, it seems that this particular one is filled with marriage ceremonies. Weddings are sentimental, happy celebrations, and it is a time for families to gather together and honor the bride and groom. A recent trip to another state to attend the wedding of some good friends' son convinced me that the only thing more memorable than an Irish wake is an Italian wedding fest.

After driving for several hours to our destination, we quickly unpacked our bags, freshened up, changed into our more presentable clothes, and left the motel for the rehearsal dinner. In the lobby were several people, obviously members of the same clan, some speaking rapidly in Italian, and all attempting to organize themselves into a caravan procession for the drive to the restaurant. The groom's mother, our friend, embraced us warmly and suggested that we follow their group to the dinner. Because my map reading skills are notoriously bad, and my husband was unable to drive and map read at the same time, we eagerly accepted her offer.

Our motorcade proceeded from the motel parking lot, and I felt like a politician en route to a rally. At every red light, the lead car would pull over to the shoulder of the road, followed by five or six cars directly behind him. All the drivers would get out of the cars, talk to each other, gesture excitedly with their hands, dash back to their cars, and take off again. It didn't seem to matter that other drivers were visibly dismayed and curious about this parade.

The dinner was wonderful, and we had the opportunity to put faces with the names we had heard for years — "Aunt Tina," "Uncle Lawrence," "Cousin Anna," "Grandmother Mary," "Sister Dorothy," "Brother Frank," and all the relatives became real to us. They were no longer just names, and stories, but personalities and animated conversationalists.

The evening of the wedding, we once more lined up our motorized procession, and traveled en masse to the church. As the members of the groom's family were seated on the right, and the bride's guests took their seats in the left pews of the church, there were nervous, curious glances being exchanged across the center aisle, and strangers were united under one roof to witness the sacred union of two separate persons into one.

With the wedding party in their designated places at the front of the church, the organist began playing the "Wedding March" as the bride came down the aisle, on the arm of her father, to join her expectant bridegroom. She, in traditional white bridal attire, and he, in the familiar formal black tuxedo, repeated the timeless vows of love, respect, and faithfulness to one another in the presence of those who gathered together.

As they stood, facing each other on the altar, their shiny gold wedding bands mirroring the stars in their eyes, I felt a familiar dampness trickling from the corners of my eyes. Embarrassed by my emotional display, I quickly smiled as I saw purses opened by every female in the first 10 pews, and tissues dabbed against teary, smiling faces.

Our motorcade traveled towards the reception hall, and after a wrong turn, a near pile-up on the interstate, and a great deal more hand waving, we arrived in time to toast the new bride and groom. We ate, danced, toasted the new couple once more, ate some more, danced some more, and became one family united in our joy for these two special young people.

The new couple drove away, their car unmistakably that of newlyweds, and the invited guests began to leave, one by one. The magic of the evening would long be remembered, and often repeated by different men and women, but each wedding would reaffirm the beauty and essence of love.

October 20, 1988

NEWLYWEDS TRAIL OF TEARS

*T*here are just some things that don't come naturally to everyone. Some of God's beautiful creatures are able to fly to majestic heights on feathered wings, some can swim effortlessly on any body of water by merely moving their little webbed feet, and others can swing from tree to tree, using long lithesome arms, legs, and a lengthy powerful tail.

Nobody expects to see a monkey swimming in a lake, a duck perched high on a tree limb, or a bird eating a banana. Yet among the human species, there seemed to be a bit of a problem when it was discovered that I, multi-talented creature that I profess to be, found it virtually impossible to execute one particular meaningless function.

I was a starry eyed young bride convinced that my new husband and I were the most perfectly suited couple that had ever been joined in matrimony. We were on the road home, returning from a week-long, blissful honeymoon in Florida, to our brand new apartment.

"Honey, sweetums, precious, would you like to stop for an ice cream cone?" my beloved asked.

"Oh, you are the sweetest, most considerate, cutest, husband that ever lived. Of course I'd love to have an ice cream cone, if you would," I replied sweetly.

He parked the car, came to the passenger side, and helped me out of the seat. I hugged his strong arm, gazed lovingly at his broad shoulders, and knew that nowhere on the face of the entire earth were there any two people any happier or more blissful than we were. What could possibly ever cause this perfect existence to go awry? I was soon to discover the answer.

"Here, Honey, since we turned off the main highway to get the ice cream, study the map, and tell me which road to take." He handed me the folded paper map, and I felt a surge of panic. I couldn't let him know that geography was my very worst subject in school, and that the little colored lines representing the highways and byways of our country made absolutely no sense at all to me. I concentrated very hard on the map in front of my bewildered eyes, and blurted out, "Take a left turn."

Thirty minutes later, he pulled over to the side of the road, gently removed the map from my sweaty tightened fists and said through clenched teeth, "You have gotten us lost."

"Well I thought we were on the right road," I whimpered.

"How in the world could anybody not see the right way to get back to the main highway? Look at this map. See how clearly it shows the access roads".

I couldn't see the map because there were huge tears forming in my formerly starry eyes. I sniffed, and told him if it was so easy to do, he should have let me drive while he read the map. We exchanged several verbal observations about the mentality of one another, and I was sure that I would take my suitcase from the trunk of our car as soon as we arrived home, and head straight for my parents' house. I'd tell them that I had been wrong to marry this man, and that I'd move back home, pawn the rings, get a job, or maybe enter the convent after all.

That incident happened 29 years ago this month. I did not move back home, needless to say, nor enter the convent, much to the relief of my parents and the good sisters. Every trip that we have taken since that time, I know that I won't be entrusted with Rand McNally's pride and joy, and when I travel the interstates around town, I always carry a large bag of breadcrumbs to scatter behind me.

February 4, 1992

PARENTS CAN'T ALWAYS FIX LIFE'S BOO-BOOS

*W*hen little ones are underfoot, it seems that Band-aids® and kisses are always in demand; the first one requiring constant replenishment, while the second's supply lasts indefinitely. Bruises, cuts, and scrapes respond quickly to Mom's healing touch, and the scars they leave behind are proudly worn like badges, with accompanying stories to embellish the accident.

The baby tips out of the walker or crawls down a step inside the house, right under Mom or Dad's vigilant eye. The newly acquired teeth hit the tender little rosebud mouth, and the tears and blood begin to flow simultaneously. Baby wails, while Mom fights her own tears, and the first of many injuries initiates the tiny warrior and his personal trainer.

Whether they are called "bah-bahs," "boo-boos," 'hurty places," or "lumpies," childhood injuries are an inevitable part of life. A burned finger from a hot stove unit will quickly teach a toddler to stay away from it in the future, but a fall from a tricycle doesn't seem to discourage it's rider from getting back in the seat, even before the scraped knee is bandaged.

When I was a little girl, I was extremely cautious, because my grandmother was a firm believer in the healing power of iodine, and had successfully convinced her daughter, my mother, to keep the medicine cabinet well stocked. It always made the injured site appear worse that it really was, by coloring the surrounding skin a horrid rusty stain, that lasted for weeks. When we fell down or got cut, we hustled to hide from that small infamous brown bottle bearing the skull and crossbones trademark, with its torturous glass wand applicator. If we weren't in pain from the injury, we knew about the added torture of the stinging medicine. Lots of small scrapes and scratches were carefully hidden from Grammie's sight, and self treated with a little unsanitary spit on a handkerchief.

As children get older, the visible little scars fade, and in the process of growing up, injuries occur that Mom and Dad cannot kiss and make all better.

The pain of a broken bone becomes nothing compared to a playmate's birthday party invitation that is never extended. A large wound can be closed with stitches, but if classmates tease your child because he is too fat, too skinny, too tall, too short, too smart, too dumb, too cute, or too ugly, there aren't enough sutures to close the injury. The stain of invisible iodine gets poured directly onto your child's ego, and you attempt to ease the sting with unsolicited parental encouragement.

There are parties and dances your child might miss, either because she isn't invited, or he chooses not to attend. In typical unbiased parental judgment, you know that your child would be the best looking person there, but there are no bandages large enough to cover the injured psyche of a slighted teenager. If he doesn't make the football team, or she doesn't get elected to the cheering squad, you make him a chocolate cake or take her shopping for a new dress to soothe some of the hurt. They've outgrown your lap, but never your heart.

Eventually Mom's kisses and Dad's words of wisdom aren't the welcome balm they once were, and some confused young adults seek relief from their hurts through unwise choices. Alcohol, drugs, "safe sex," and pressure from misguided peers lure them with the promise of comfort and freedom from pain. These temptations replace the band aids, and might work for a while, until they fall off, exposing a deeper and ever festering invisible laceration.

Hopefully, they begin to make their own place in the world, and just as surely as they touched that hot stove, they are going to get burned by people, places, and circumstances that occur in their lives. Some of them never learned the difference between leaving the stove alone, and getting back on that harmless tricycle for another ride. You watch as they make apparent judgment errors, and pray that their spirits can take as much bruising as their tender little limbs once did.

Dreams and hearts can so easily be broken, but love is the plaster cast that helps them to mend again.

March 16, 1993

BEING A TWOSOME MEANS LETTING GO
OF LIFE A LITTLE

I alternated between crying and laughing, starving and stuffing, feeling calm and fighting off persistent internal butterflies. I thought I was a pro, and that my previous experiences had prepared me for the impending event. For the third, and final (please, Lord) time, I was going to be the mother of the groom. It should have been a breeze, but there was one slight disruptive factor I hadn't fully comprehended. This was the baby, the last of our brood to take that final step from hearth, home, Mom and Dad.

When we married, our generation really didn't know about career choices or family planning. We fell, contentedly, into the stereotypical, young Catholic couple lifestyle, and the two of us were soon the three, four and five of us. By, the time I was 27, and my husband 28 years old, our last child, (now this prospective bridegroom), was born. As a result of having our family rather early, we never had much time to be a twosome. Cooking was always done in quantities, and as economically as possible. Cleaning was done in a frenzy; usually late at night after baths and bedtime stories, and decorating the house was a matter of practicality rather than aesthetic value. How well I remember the horrified look on our builder's face when I chose all natural woodwork throughout our new home. Red tricycles and black rubber tires on large metal trucks really didn't mix well with gloss white trim.

Now this last child of ours was going to take a wife of his own, as his two older brothers had done, and we are faced with the reality that we are finally alone together. Fortunately, we have communicated very well, (silently, tenderly, loudly and emphatically), with each other during the past 34 years, so we are not experiencing "getting to know one another." No, we are in the dilemma of what to do with the rest of our adult lives, now that we are free of the responsibility of child rearing; just when we were beginning to get the hang of it, too.

Should we board the dog indefinitely, and become beach bums in Hawaii? Throw all caution to the wind and take up wind surfing, parasailing, hang gliding, hot air balloon riding, roller blades, or bungee jumping? Our arthritis screams "you'd better not," and we wisely listen. Will we be destined to spend our mature (hate the word) adult life watching the weather channel and "dancing Grannies" exercise tapes, prowling the local restaurants for early dinner and senior citizen discount meals, and waiting for the mailman?

Now that we have arrived at the time in our lives when an occasional steak dinner wouldn't destroy a month's budget, we find out that beef and fat are our arteries' worst enemies. We throw out half loaves of fuzzy green bread, and cautiously sniff and check the date on a quart of skim milk. In spite of our valiant efforts at dietary reformation, the only thing about us that gets thinner is our hair. The dishwasher needs to be run only a couple of times a week, instead of hourly, and the washer and dryer, on their maiden "gentle" and "mini" cycles, no longer hum round the clock. We are the only people on our block that carry on lengthy conversations with the carpet cleaning and cemetery plot telemarketers, and we each appreciate the luxury of our own private bathrooms.

The wedding guests are all seated, and I take many deep breaths as I am ushered into my seat by our other two sons. There is a sharp ache in my shoulders, as I fight to keep the tears inside. I look at the groom, standing beside his father/best man, and I see a nostalgic, handsome reflection of my own youthful bridegroom. The beautiful, radiant bride is escorted down the aisle by her father, who is also taking deep breaths, valiantly struggling for his composure. We, the four proud parents, rejoice in their union, and are overcome with emotion.

"For better or worse, for richer or poorer, in sickness and in health, till death do us part," is repeated solemnly by the bride and groom, and re-affirmed silently within my heart as I recall;

"Grow old along with me, the best is yet to be, the last of life, for which the first was made. Our times are in His hand."

May 1, 1993

MOTHER'S DAY TELLS STORY OF LOVE; FOUND AND FORGOTTEN

They got married in January 1963. Four months later, on the second Sunday in May, she got a big, beautiful flowery card from her husband that was to "My Wonderful Wife on Mothers' Day". Next to his signature, was a small paw imprint of their new puppy.

May 1964. Her card had a kitten on the front of it and was for the "Mommy To Be". It was signed "with love from ?" and she pasted it in the baby book, along with one of the yellow baby bootie shower invitations.

In May of 1966, she got a card from "Mommie's Little Boy," complete with a forged lopsided printed signature, and she announced to her mother and mother-in-law that they would be grandmothers again by winter.

On Mother's Day in 1969, her son gave her a plaster of paris wall hanging of his little hand print. He had made it in kindergarten and sprayed it with gold paint. Her toddler daughter had scribbled on a card that read to "Mom From Her Little Helper." Their father had taken them to the drugstore to shop for gifts, and they chose a bottle of dark red nail polish, a kite, and a pair of yellow plastic hoop earrings.

By May of 1973, the twins had arrived, and she got a card from "All Of Us," on which her son had signed his neat cursive script, and her daughter had printed her name with a green crayon. The two identical infant boys had to depend on Dad to add their names. She had hinted that she wanted a printed cotton "muumuu" to wear when she took the kids to swim practice.

Her husband proudly presented her with a chartreuse lace teddie, complete with matching feather boa, that he had ordered from a well known, mail order lingerie catalog.

In 1980, her son raced out of the house a little before noon on that Sunday in May, jumped in his new used car, and headed for the store. He came back with a card for "Someone who's Been Like A Mother To Me," and wrote a brief note beneath his signature, declaring "this was all that was left — Sorry." Her daughter had served her an oatmeal and orange juice breakfast, with a handmade card, on the bed tray to "The World's Best Mother." The twins had relied on their father for their contribution to the collection, but had each painstakingly printed their own names. They gave her a donut maker.

In 1982, everyone forgot that it was Mother's Day, so she pouted all morning, waiting for cards and remembrances that never materialized. By nightfall, when someone realized what day it was, and told the others, they offered to take her out for pizza, but she declined and went to bed early. She called the beauty shop for an appointment on Monday, and bought herself a hot fudge sundae on the way home.

The following year, there was no word from her son who was "finding himself," after dropping out of college. The twins, disregarding her diet, gave her a box of chocolates, and a bakery decorated cake. Her daughter, wearing too much make-up and cheap jewelry, was off to meet her undesirable boyfriend when she handed her mother a letter:

"Dear Mom, Hope you have a good Mother's Day. When I get paid on Thursday, I'll buy you a new purse. Yours looks gross."

(She approved so much of the one she bought; she "borrowed" it from her mother the next week, along with the money for a new prom dress.)

"Happy Mother's Day From Both Of Us," arrived in May 1986, signed by her oldest son and his yet unseen new bride. They were both away in school, and he had finally gotten a haircut. He lectured his frustrated parents on how to discipline the adventuresome twins, now both 13. From her daughter, she accepted a lengthy, collect long distance phone call which ended in angry tears for both parties. She also got a hot air popcorn popper, and a personalized ceramic coffee mug.

She turned off the cordless weed eater that her husband had given her, when the florist truck pulled into the driveway. The elaborate bouquet from her son arrived the day before Mother's Day 1992. The attached card bore only his signature, and she realized that his divorce was now a reality. The mailman handed her a computer chip musical card, from one of the twins, with an "insufficient postage due" notice stamped beneath the out of state postmark. When she opened it "Love Me Tender" serenaded her. Also arriving that Saturday was a pink envelope, addressed in her daughter's neat familiar scrawl. The enclosed card proclaimed "Happy Mother's Day To My Grandma," signed with X's, and O's. Through her tears she read the surprise announcement inside, "I'll be arriving Christmas. Love, ?"

February 8, 2015

SHOW SOME LOVE EACH DAY

*A*dvertisements are filled with pictures of hearts, red and white stuffed animals, flowers, perfume, candy, jewelry, and greeting cards. In an attempt to get people to want, and others to buy, these items for Valentine's Day, the retailers began putting up displays immediately after all the marked down Christmas items were removed from prominent shelves and banished to a more obscure aisle. They want to entice shoppers to show their love for others by purchasing a gift for that special someone. The donor gets brownie points for doing something good, and the merchants show a profit for February. It's a win-win situation.

It's fun to receive Valentine cards, and I do my share of mailing them out every year to let those I care about know it. Every year, I sent a card to my in-laws for every occasion, and after the death of my mother-in-law, I continued sending them to my husband's father. After years of never acknowledging any of them, I decided to just stop, launching my strike on a particular Valentine Day. Late that afternoon, I got a phone call from our very own Archie Bunker clone. "What happened? Did your mailman die?" I asked why, and he told me in his own charming way that he didn't get a Valentine card from us. I replied, "No, because I thought you didn't want them since you never mentioned the many that have previously been sent." He growled, "Well, I do" and hung up the phone. From that day on, I resumed sending the cards like clockwork, never receiving any more feedback from him, but assuming he was pleased to get them. After he passed away, we found bundles of the opened cards, tucked away in the bottom of his sock drawer; proof that even curmudgeons want to know they are loved by others.

Wouldn't it be nice to show love to others the remaining 364 days out of the year? We don't have to always send a card or give a gift to convey our feelings, but can search for creative ways to show someone you care about them, and that they matter in your life. There is a new commercial that I saw for the first time during Super Bowl Sunday. It shows a bottle of a well known cola drink getting accidentally spilled down into the inside workings of a massive computer, shorting out wires and creating havoc with everything electronic. When the glitch kicks in, in the flash of an eye, two men who are in a heated argument on a television show are magically transformed into buddies happily chatting with each other. A young boy is on a school bus when he gets a text message that reads "nobody likes you." Looking around to try and discover the sender's identity, the message changes to state "there's nobody like you", which brings a smile to his face, rather than a tear to his eye or a pain to his heart.

In 1965, Burt Bacharach and Hal David collaborated on a song entitled "What The World Needs Now." Jackie DeShannon recorded it, and it climbed to the number seven spot on the most popular song lists that year. The simple opening lyrics of "What the world needs now is love sweet love, it's the only thing that there's just too little of" are timeless, and just as true now as they were half a century ago. The song has been recorded by more than 100 other artists over the years, and used as the sound track in several movies.

Stevie Wonder wrote, produced and recorded his number one Billboard Hot 100 hit, "I Just Called To Say I Love You." Remaining at the top of the charts for three weeks in 1984, Stevie proclaims in the chorus of this song, "I just called to say I love you. I just called to say how much I care. I just called to say I love you, and I mean it from the bottom of my heart." Sounds so simple, doesn't it?

Although it's idealistic and often difficult, just think of how much the world would improve if we could just make every day Valentine's Day. Just call and say "I love you" to someone. Maybe it will spread faster than any virus ever known to mankind.

TAKE TWO ASPIRIN AND PLEASE DON'T CALL ME IN THE MORNING

Chapter

January 16, 1990

TAKE TWO ASPIRIN

*I*t started out simply enough; a congested feeling in my chest, signaling an approaching cold. Everyone seemed to either have the flu bug, or was just getting over it, and from the stories I'd heard, it just didn't appeal to me to be at the mercy of those nasty germs.

By the time supper was over, I knew the congestion was getting worse, and I headed for the nearest drugstore.

"I'll drive you up there to the store," my husband kindly offered. I gratefully accepted, wondering if I should pick up some aspirin, magazines, ginger ale, tissues, and pineapple sherbet to sustain me during the impending illness.

"I'll just run in and pick up some cough syrup. It'll only take a few minutes," I told him.

Twenty minutes later, he came in the store, looking exasperated with me.

"What in the world are you doing standing here in front of the cough syrup? Just get some and let's get out of here"

"I can't," I whimpered.

"What do you mean, 'you can't?' What's the big problem getting a little bottle of cough syrup?"

"I need my reading glasses to read the labels of all these bottles," I explained.

"Why do you have to read all of them, just pick out the one you want, and I'll read it to you."

"I can read the big letters, if I stand way back over here by the bandaids; one is for congestion with a cough, one is for congestion without a cough, one is for stuffy nose, one is to dry up a runny nose, one is for ... where are you going?"

He returned promptly with my glasses, and we started reading all the various labels on the long row of brown cough syrup bottles.

"I think I've got it," I shouted.

"What does it say?"

"For the relief of chest congestion without coughs, without fever, without sinus infection, without headaches, and no symptoms of influenza present. What do you think?"

"Sounds perfect for you — is it your right size?" he asked.

"I don't know about this. I have a slight headache, and I feel little chilled-could be flu symptoms and that would exclude me from eligibility for this brand."

Pointing out that my headache was probably a result of 30 minutes of intensive research on over the counter cough remedies, I was prepared to make my decision.

"Wait a minute," I mumbled as we headed for the check out line.

"What's the matter now?"

"This one is just for night time coughs. What if I need it during the day?"

"How's it gonna know if you're taking it in the day or night?"

"The label says not to operate machinery, or drive a car, and it also says it might make me drowsy," I answered, pointing to the tiny print on the back of the package.

After reading more labels, we made a careful decision as to what I should do for my congestion.

Reeking of menthol, I headed for the comfort of the sofa, steaming cup in my hand. I washed down the two aspirin with the warm hot toddy, confident that I'd made a wise choice.

However, if my symptoms change within 24 hours, I'll have to return to the drugstore and seek out a more appropriate remedy. Maybe I should pack a lunch.

February 5, 1991

The Flu Bug:
An Unwelcome Guest That Won't Leave

f a bug gets in your home and won't vacate the premises, despite all efforts, an exterminator can usually manage to get the pest out. Not so if the "bug" happens to be a virus that attacks the body. No amount of medicine can force the stubborn invader to surrender its hold on the invisible human immune system.

I caught a bug, or rather, it caught me recently. The onset of the critter seemed innocent enough. Mild stomach distress, which I attributed to spicy foods. The mild distress quickly became the focus of my attention, as I attempted to ignore it by shopping. It caused me to search desperately for the nearest restroom in a department store where none were visible. After frantic inquiries of skeptical sales personnel, I gratefully located the inner sanctum of "employees only" facilities, and returned to the business of scouring the mark down racks. Once more, the ugly monster attacked my inner digestive track, bringing a clammy feeling to my skin, and a dizziness to my head not associated with unbelievable bargains. I sipped on a cola, and sent secret messages to the bug that it wasn't welcome, and to please go bother someone else.

By evening, the bug was growing stronger, and attacking the parts of my body that created sneezes, sniffles, and all sorts of other undesirable cold symptoms. Out came the boxes of tissues, the decongestant, nose drops, vaporizer, aspirin, flannel gown, and lots of liquids. The war was on between me and this bug, and I was determined to win.

Coughing, sneezing, and feeling generally miserable, I attempted to sleep. The bug was wide awake, and determined not to be alone, so it clogged my airways, and invaded my mind with thousands of those random thoughts that keep one awake all night. I tried lying on my side, my back, my stomach, more pillows, no pillows, more covers, less covers, reading, hot herbal tea, and more aspirin. No use, I switched on late night television, and was promptly absorbed in Wolf Blitzer and Charles Jaco's accounts of Desert Storm. The early morning hours found me still sniffling, my cold symptoms worse, and my depression increasing. I drug myself out of bed, reasoning that work would cause me to forget my state of illness.

The bug wasn't happy at work either, it made me want to make a pallet on the floor of the office, and stay on break for several hours. As soon as I came home, I headed for the bed, and once more resumed my CNN vigil, chicken soup in hand. This routine repeated itself for a week, and by the time the week-end rolled around, I was weaning myself off the disturbing war news, and onto 1940 color enhanced John Wayne war movies. The bug seemed to be packing up its gear, heading for fresh territory, and I finally felt the welcome relief of sleep approaching.

The bug put down its suitcases, decided it liked the surroundings, and proceeded to invite several members of its family to spend a few days. They sent chills to all parts of my body, signaling fresh attacks.

My body was too weak to resist the invaders, so they once more took over, and eagerly consumed all the home remedies I fed them, growing stronger, instead of weaker as they were supposed to. A phone call to the doctor, and a prescription later, I swallowed some large pink pills that I hoped would overtake the pesky bug. I envisioned little pink pac men chasing the invader, and its kin-folk, through my blood stream, and out of my body for good.

The pink pac men made me feel worse, but I continued sending them on their missions. I got fever, more chills, and a fresh batch of cold symptoms. By now, I had forsaken Charles, Wolf, and the Duke for soap operas and Vanna White, assuming that my mind needed a rest to rid me of the stubborn bug. I was starting to feel that I was a candidate for exorcism, but instead settled for an office visit to my physician.

After three weeks of horrendous suffering and nastiness, and countless failed attempts to evict the bug, I felt all of my symptoms vanish as I awaited the doctor's appearance in the treatment room. No cough, no chills, no fever, not one sign of the wretched beast could be found as the cold stethoscope listened for the wheezing in my chest. My "cure" lasted until I got back home, and the illusive creature seized me once more.

Perhaps I'll just name it and claim it as a dependent on our income tax return.

January 6, 1993

MENTHOLATUM, EUCALYPTUS AND THE TENNESSEE CRUD

They call it the "Tennessee Crud," and it is not a new Southern drink recipe, a popular tourist attraction, or a thoroughbred horse. I feel certain that it is not confined to our part of the country, and it has nothing to do with Johnny Majors, Phil Fulmer, Lamar Alexander, Ned Ray McWherter, or the Hall of Fame football victory. Well, nothing unless some, or all, of these more prominent residents happen to have fallen victim to the latest "bug" that seems to have invaded every home, office, school, church, and hospital in the entire state.

My personal bout with the awfulness began the first week of December. It started with a very unattractive drippy nose for one entire day, progressed into a sore throat, coughing, and eventually, laryngitis. I don't do well when I lose my voice, but my family loves it. I try whispering, but nobody pays attention to me; come to think of it, they don't pay any more attention to me when I'm yelling my head off. My telephone voice sounded like I just woke up, and when I called my answering machine to leave verbal memos to myself, I wondered who I was when I listened to the playback. I felt rotten, looked pale, and resorted to charade gestures for communication; I resembled a mime artist without a beret.

It wasn't exactly a cold, and it wasn't like the flu. (Couldn't be the flu anyway, I took the shot, I reasoned.) Antibiotics didn't seem to help eliminate the symptoms, and it didn't make me feel bad enough to retreat to bed for several days with hot tea, soda crackers, and a comfy old quilt. I just drug through the days, feeling crummy, hoping it wouldn't last much longer. Dozens of boxes of tissue, and several days passed, and the wretched invisible intruder was still residing inside my chest, throat, and head. All throughout the Christmas holidays, I carried a box of tissue and a bottle of cough syrup wherever I went, and everyone thought I was Rudolph's twin sister. I gratefully gulped down either nasty tasting, fizzy cold relief medicine or even worse tasting liquid night time

179

remedy. Grogginess overtook me, and I slept for a few hours, only to wake up in the wee hours of the morning, unable to breathe — a very serious obstacle to restful slumber. Recalling Grandma's favorite remedy from my childhood, I applied great globs of menthol rub to my wheezing chest, and stole undershirts from my husband's dresser drawer to wear over the greasy residue.

Weeks passed, and I alternated between feeling better and worse. My voice came and went, and I spoke in husky, squeaky short sentences. The cough appeared at very inconvenient times of the day and night, and proved to be stronger than any of the medications I sent to conquer it. My breath reeked of eucalyptus cough drops, and a trip to the drugstore became my daily ritual.

"Have you had this awful virus thing that's going around," I asked a friend.

"Oh, yes, and it's just miserable. Stomach cramps, nausea, chills, and a killer headache," she replied.

"Wait a minute, you don't have the runny nose, watery eyes, chest congestion, itchy ears, coughing, sneezing, month and a half 'bug,' do you? You've got a different ..."

She cut me off with her quickly mumbled response of "gotta go — bathroom," and slammed down the phone.

Just as the last traces of the strange malady are leaving me, and I think I am over the worst of it, a devastating new complication develops.

"Do we hab any more of dat medicine youb ben taking?" my husband sniffled. The laundry room will reek of menthol coated undershirts hastily put in the washer and dryer.

January 29, 1997

Taking Care Of Sick People Used To Be Much Simplier

The thermometer was removed from my mouth, and as she held it up to the light to get an accurate reading, a look of concern was on my mother's face. I knew before she told me that I had a fever. The chills, body aches and general overall bad feeling alerted my 12-year-old body to that undeniable fact.

She headed for the phone, made her call to our kind pediatrician, and then she proceeded to go into her housekeeping mode.

"Get up and take a bath, while I change your sheets and vacuum the room," she directed.

The last thing I wanted to do was leave the snug and comfortable confines of my bed, and to climb into the bathtub was certainly not high on my list of desires at this moment. Knowing that resisting would be futile, I made my way to the bathroom. After drying off, I was ready to put my well worn flannel gown back on, when the door opened, and Mamma threw in a clean pair of ironed cotton pajamas.

"Here, put these on, brush your teeth, comb your hair, and come on back here and get into bed before Dr. Weaver arrives for his house call."

May I interject at this point in my story that the words "house call" may seem unfamiliar terminology to some readers, and I will make a brief attempt to enlighten those who are confused. Doctors used to come to the homes of patients who were too ill to make it to the office. If a patient needed medical attention after office hours, instead of heading for the emergency room of the closest hospital, their physician would answer his own telephone at his home and make the trip to the patient's bedside. No, they didn't come in a horse and buggy. They drove automobiles, and generally responded quickly to the patient's situation.

In our case, Dr. Weaver lived only a few blocks from our house, so he was always gracious about stopping on his way home from the office, or coming over to bring down a late night fever, or calm a croupy cough and worried parents. He would come in the house, carrying his well worn black leather bag, pull out his stethoscope, tongue depressors, flashlight, and thermometer, and begin his bedside exam after carefully washing his hands. He was always given the distinct privilege of using the guest towels reserved for company and a fresh bar of soap.

"Deep breath," he would admonish as the cold stethoscope pressed against a feverish chest and back.

"Say 'ah,'" he requested, as the tongue depressor was guided to the back of one's mouth, followed by the inevitable gagging reflex.

Next the eyes, nose, and ears were checked with the aid of his special light, and then the reflexes, neck rigidity, and tenderness in the abdominal region were noted. Most often the diagnose's was a virus, or, as in my case this time, an upper respiratory infection, and a sample dose of antibiotic was dispensed along with a prescription to be filled in the morning. He didn't believe in giving aspirin in the presence of a fever, because he felt it would "mask the symptoms," but baby aspirin were deemed ok for aches and pains in the absence of fever.

He was not an exception in the matter of making house calls during a time when doctors catered to the patient's needs. Most families had a pediatrician and a family doctor that were very involved in treating any ailment or malady that might befall a member of the household. They were pre-HMO, PPO, managed care, Medicare, non-aspirin pain relievers, primary providers, HIPPA, walk-in clinics, co-pay, and deductibles. There was no referral, approval, list of approved care givers or criteria that had to be met. If a doctor met with one's approval, they were usually bonded to that patient for life, and often extended their care to the next generation. Many times, awakened from slumber in late evening hours, a doctor would justifiably respond with the familiar phrase "take two aspirin and call me in the morning" to eliminate the need for an unscheduled house call. While some abused the convenience of house calls, most patients respected the physician's schedule and reserved this ritual for severe symptoms or critical situations.

Mamma used it as an excuse for getting our bedrooms presentable.

February 11, 1997

TLC: SICKIES NEED HAS GIVEN WAY TO HIGH EFFICIENCY

*B*ecause there are no longer doctors who make house calls for ailing patients, it has become necessary for the patients to schedule a visit to the doctor's office for diagnosis and treatment, or utilize the closest walk-in emergency clinic. It would be a gross understatement to say that this can sometimes be a very frustrating experience.

If the malady starts out with a common cold, most people will postpone calling for medical intervention and rely on aspirin, fluids, dozens of tissues, and a bit of TLC. My cold did not respond to any of the above, and I developed a very unattractive and sleep interrupting cough. I reluctantly decided that it was time to quit sniffling, sneezing and complaining and begin to feel human again.

I dialed my physician's office number, the telephone rang, and a pleasant voice responded;

"Dr. I. Treatum's office, how may I help you?"

"Well, I have this rotten cold, and ..."

"Do you have fever?"

"Gee, I don't have a thermometer, but I feel like I might. You know how you get chills one minute and ..."

"Hold please for the phone nurse."

I am placed on hold and listen to classical music for several minutes before I hear another voice on the line.

"Mrs. Lambert, are you having problems?"

I begin to recite my complaints, and wait to elicit a sympathetic response.

"We need to get you in for a chest X-ray; hold on while I connect you to the appointment secretary."

Again I listen to the musical interlude while I wait for the next human contact.

"Our first available appointment for your X-ray and follow up with the doctor is next Tuesday afternoon. Be here at 2:15. By the way, we are in our new office at Mega Medical Center South, and I'll send you a map with directions."

I have taken road trips with maps less involved than the one I received in the mail. I follow the directions and arrive at a small skyscraper building. After guiding the car up several levels of a winding parking garage, a narrow vacant spot is spied, and the car is carefully maneuvered into it. It is a snug fit, leaving little room to open the car door and ease out, and the word "contortionist" takes on a whole new meaning. Limbo contests have been won by people with less agility than it takes to vacate the driver's seat.

The nearest elevator is at the other end of the floor, a nice little jaunt when one feels fit, but a cross country journey when accompanied by body aches. The elevator door shuts, and the choice of mezzanine, balcony, basement, lobby, main entrance, or skywalk must be decided. Gambling on main entrance seems safe, and once there, it becomes necessary to walk to another set of elevators which transports me to the various floors of the medical plaza. I am wondering at this point if I should have been dropping bread crumbs to find my way back.

I arrive on time for the appointment, and after signing in at the desk, I produce proof of my insurance to the receptionist. One hour later, I am escorted to the inner sanctum of the treatment area, given a lovely paper, immodest hospital gown, and led to the X-ray room. After my photo session, I, along with my handbag and clothing, am placed in a patient exam room, where I catch a nap while awaiting the doctor's arrival.

"X-rays are clear. Let me listen to your chest now. Hmm ... sounds ok. Ears, nose, throat — say 'ah' — are a little irritated. Let's put you on a round of antibiotics for a week. Check back when you've finished them if you don't feel better."

He scribbles on a prescription pad, hands it to the nurse, and is gone before I can say a word. I put my clothes back on, and mentally try to prepare myself for the return trip to the car. Was I on the yellow armadillo, green cricket, pink kiwi, blue daisy, or purple bullfrog level of the parking garage?

After a lengthy search, I finally locate the car, do my Houdini impression of re-entering it, and head for the drugstore, where I wait in a long line to get my prescription filled. Fifty-two dollars poorer, I discover after taking the third dose of the medication I am allergic to it, and must get an alternate prescription, which is more expensive but better tolerated. Noting that the cure is worse than the ailment, I feel wretched.

Life was indeed so much simpler when we took two aspirins and called in the morning.

January 10, 2015

DAYTIME TV IS TORTURE

The sub-freezing temperatures all across the United States have given us the assurance of a fact we already knew, but didn't want to admit: Old Man Winter has taken up his annual residence. Freezing pipes, snow storms, frozen ponds, homeless shelters filled to capacities, school buses that refuse to start, multi-layers of warm clothing, and a strong desire to hibernate until warmer weather are the norm. And along with all of those indicators of winter's presence, there is one other very unwelcome trend that brings us untold amounts of discomfort and suffering.

The flu has made its appearance once more, and despite a vaccine which apparently does not protect its recipients from the particular strain of influenza that is running rampant, the numbers of those affected continues to grow. While I hesitate to even say it, we have been fortunate thus far in escaping that nasty little flu bug, but we have acquired some other stubborn malady that seems to be going around.

It started on Christmas Eve for my husband with a sore throat. We were able to entertain our family, but by Christmas night, he was confined to his recliner, coughing, and feeling generally lousy. Sapped of any amount of energy, he ate, slept and pretty much took up residence in the confines of his chair for several days. Repeated requests for temperature checks failed to show any results other than normal, but after such a lengthy bout of the upper respiratory mess, his physician took pity on him and sent a couple of prescriptions which successfully attacked and wounded the bug. Meanwhile, I was overdosing on much more than the minimum required dosage of Vitamin C, bleaching everything in the house and trying to ward off the illness.

Just as he was showing some signs of improvement, and I was beginning to resemble a pumpkin from the excessive vitamin intake, I evicted him from his nest, laid in a huge supply of tissues, and picked up the coughing torch. Nothing seemed to make it any better. I tried sitting, laying down, propped up on dozens of pillows. I drank hot tea and honey in massive quantities, sucked on cough drops constantly, and slathered large quantities of menthol medicated rub on my feet, chest, back, and neck. With socks on my feet, tee shirt under my night gown, cold drainage in both eyes, and reeking of menthol ointment, I was a sight bad enough to merely scare any germs out of our house, but they were evidently blinded by my beauty, and stubbornly refused to leave.

My exercise routine consisted of putting a load of clothes in the washer, and then lay down for a nap. Put the clothes in the dryer, then take another nap. My energy was non-existent, and the mere thought of doing any much needed housework sent me into a semi-comatose state. We ate so much chicken soup, I felt that we would both soon grow feathers and crow at daybreak.

With my body refusing to move, I was a captive audience for daytime television shows. If I thought the chest cold was bad, it quickly became apparent that our government could utilize network televisions shows, during the daytime hours, as the most severe type of punishment for captives. After three hours of game and talk shows, anyone would give up even the most secure national secrets to have the television silenced.

There are shows depicting the daily lives of hoarders, polygamists, home improvement wizards, and people who clip enough coupons to actually get thousands of dollars worth of groceries for less than a dollar. I am mesmerized as I watch "reality" shows, but would be amazed if Honey Boo Boo's family and Kate with her brood of eight will survive another season. The soap opera that I haven't followed for 10 years re-entered my life, and I got caught up on the latest happenings within the first two days of viewing. The commercials advertise products that claim to cure every disease known to mankind, and if you can ignore the numerous side effects they quickly skim through, it would seem that there should not be any illness in the world that isn't curable with a pill.

As the days passed, and my symptoms finally subsided, I was able to wean myself off of television, and menthol rub, and to create a noticeable decline in the sale of disposable tissues. Lest I follow in the footsteps of the infamous Typhoid Mary, please don't think I'm rude if I decline a handshake. It might just contain our remote control.

February 10, 2014

HOSPITAL ENCOUNTERS
OF THE CLOSEST KIND

Every person we meet has a story to tell. As we rush from place to place every day, we pass by amazing human beings without having the time or inclination to learn about the struggles, dreams, accomplishments, or challenges that someone other than ourselves faces. But occasionally, God puts us in a position to interact with others on a deeper level of conversation. It is always surprising what we can learn if we only take the time to listen.

This occurs on a daily basis in countless hospitals across the world. As we sit in waiting rooms for hours, awaiting news about the outcome of surgery on a friend or loved one, we find ourselves passing the anxious moments by asking those around us about the circumstances that brought them to this institute. Recently, I found myself in this situation while awaiting the outcome of my husband's surgery.

As the nurses prepped my husband for surgery, I was led to a small "pre-op" waiting room, where one designated family member or friend could wait to see their patient just prior to their operation. I entered the room of strangers and found an empty chair. I had brought along some yarn and a crochet needle so I could occupy myself with some mindless distraction as the day wore on. The shrill ring of a telephone broke the silence of the room. The woman seated closest to it attempted to answer it, but only got a dial tone in response. We unanimously elected her to be the official answerer. Repeated ringing produced the same dysfunctional results, so she decided to wait until after the second ring to pick up the receiver. I jokingly commented that it must be a telemarketer, and we began to converse with each other.

I learned that the attractive lady seated to my left was there with her husband. They suspected a malignancy in his arm and he was advised to act quickly after getting a second opinion for what was thought to be an innocent cyst by his small town general practitioner. They had driven into Nashville from their

187

home and spent several days with a relative while awaiting word of an opening in the surgeon's busy schedule. With little more than a 24-hour notice, they were summoned to the hospital. She told me they were both retired school teachers and had plans to travel. Those plans would have to be put on hold until they knew the prognosis and recommended treatment for him.

The woman directly across the room asked that we remember her nephew in our prayers. At only 24 years of age, he had undergone multiple surgeries for a rare type of cancer, and was currently preparing to undergo a procedure designed to decrease the amount of pain he was experiencing. She told us that despite his bleak prognosis and many hospitalizations, he remained optimistic and cheerful.

"My sister is here to undergo a lengthy medical treatment," chimed in a quiet girl with long red hair. She explained that the "baby" sister in a family of six other adult sisters and one brother had come to this particular hospital from another state, and it was expected that she would remain in Nashville for approximately three months as an out-patient. They had secured a small apartment close to the hospital, and each sibling would take turns traveling to Nashville from various other cities to stay with their sister.

A somewhat disheveled looking young man, reluctant to join in the impromptu group sharing, blurted out that his mother suffered from a rare form of a disease that he neither understood nor could pronounce. He was terrified of what might happen to her, but hopeful that the renowned surgeon who was doing her surgery would be able to insure a future for her. He didn't have a car, but got a friend to drive him to the hospital and was riding a bus home later that day.

I marveled at these people, some of whom had traveled many miles to seek a cure, a miracle for someone they loved. They were willing to sacrifice the comforts of their homes, their time, and whatever financial resources they might be able to obtain just to help out and give hope to their beloved patient.

As the long hours of that day and several consecutive ones wore on, and we were scattered throughout the hospital, we would greet one another in the hospital corridors, the cafeteria, or the busy lobby. We would inquire about the outcome of the surgery and assure each other of ongoing prayers for strength and recovery.

I suggest that the words of William Butler Yeats be framed to hang in every hospital waiting room: "There are no strangers here; only friends you haven't yet met."

RAINBOWS AND LOLLIPOPS

Chapter

September 18, 1986

RADIO'S MAGIC NOSTALGIA TRIP

*L*istening to the radio while preparing dinner, I tuned the volume up as I heard the famous '50s beat accompanied by Mickey Gilley singing his hit, "Doo Wah Days." It goes, in part, "back in the 'doo-wah' days, when we were young, life was a carousel; we fell in love." Nostalgia transported me back to my teen-aged years.

Memories of dances, sorority parties and outings, slumber(less) parties, plays, classes, and the main Sunday night social event of our era, CYO Teen Town, where my friends and I supported the gym wall, waiting for some brave blue jean clad fellow to saunter over and invite one of us to dance.

We really did wear those poodle skirts, with sugar stiffened crinoline petticoats to hold them out, and wide elastic cinch belts to nip in our waists. The outfits were completed with a neck scarf, blouse with turned up collar, saddle oxfords accompanied by plump rolled-down bobby socks, and our hair caught up in a sassy pony tail. When we attended a formal dance, it was a real engineering feat to fit two or three couples into someone's family car — only a select fortunate few had their own autos — as the girls had on voluminous gowns, fortified underneath by hoop skirts. Many of our mothers made our dresses, or had them made, and the basic white sorority presentation gown became the foundation for various changes of trim, as the seasonal event dictated. Only the most daring would be bold enough to defy the dear nuns regulation "three inch wide" straps, and appear in a shockingly strapless creation. It was grounds for expulsion.

The era of the '50s is in right now. Our music, clothes, memorabilia of Elvis, and the popular "rock-n-roll," all made famous by my generation. We are sometimes stereotyped as care-free, happy Ricky Nelson or Sandra Dee clones.

It seems difficult to imagine that we dealt with a great deal of frustration and anxiety, not unlike those of today. We had problem skin that always seemed to blossom at the most inopportune times, conflicts over parental authority, peer pressure, waiting for a special someone to call for a date, and hassles over grades. We were all too aware of the threat of nuclear holocaust, as we were required to wear dogtag style I.D.s, and fallout shelters became a frequent addition to many suburban yards and homes. Alcohol, sex, and crime were some of the ageless temptations we faced and dealt with, even then.

Blessedly my mind chooses to focus on the positive, fun-filled times of my youth, perhaps even embellishes on those a bit. How fortunate that human nature, being what it is, can allow us to forget the unpleasant experiences we endure, making them less painful in intensity, and permits us to magnify the pleasurable moments of our lives.

It matters not who, or what, conjures up memories of your "Doo-Wah" days, be it Sinatra, Glenn Miller, Kingston Trio, Beatles, Elvis or Lynyrd Skynyrd. When you hear "Stardust," "Goodnight, Sweetheart," "Yellow Brick Road," "Proud Mary," "Yesterday," "Moonlight Serenade," or "Free Bird," feed your imagination well. Each of us has, within the confines of our hearts and souls, an image of a personal Camelot, and as you may recall the rain never fell, and the sun always shone brightly for "happily, ever aftering" in that mythical, magical spot.

November 30, 1986

RETURN OF THE IRONING BOARD

O f all the distasteful, socially unacceptable four letter words in the English languages I find the one that is most repulsive to my delicate ears is spelled I-R-O-N.

I realize that this chore is a necessary part of personal grooming and essential to one's neat appearance. I also realize there are people in this world who do not object to pressing clothes; there are even those who enjoy this task, some of whom are personal friends. To me it is sheer torture to stand at a ironing board, or more appropriately "bored," and labor for hours on a garment which will look worse after I've struggled to make it look presentable.

When my younger brother wanted a toy iron and ironing board for Christmas one year, my aunt overrode my father's objections and saw to it that he got his wish. He would set up his little board in our basement and mimic our experienced housekeeper as she sprinkled all the clothes on the morning of each laundry day. She had a water filled soft drink bottle corked with a perforated top, which dispensed just the right amount of liquid to dampen each article of clothing. They were rolled, put into a plastic bag and allowed to season in the refrigerator until after lunch. She made a few attempts at teaching me to properly iron a man's shirt, but finally determined it was hopeless.

When polyester was the miracle fabric of the century, I was delighted. Every article of clothing my family and I wore was popped out of a dryer, hung on a hanger, and ready to wear. The fact that it was unbearably non-porous during the hot summer was of little consequence. Never mind that the amount of static electricity generated from one skirt, worn with a nylon slip, could have lit up Times Square. It was wrinkle-free at all times, and it was fashioned into fabrics that resembled wool, cotton, denim, and even silk. Dry cleaning bills took a sharp and rapid decline, while the sale of fabric softener spiraled upward. Ah, the marvels of the modern textile industry.

As with all fashion trends, the era of double knits passed, and the mercantile merchants joined in a conspiracy, with the dry cleaning industry, to saturate the American public with the latest fabric rage; cotton. This all natural fiber, which was the mainstay of generations past, was being re-introduced to the 20th century. Gradually garments, proudly displaying their "100 percent natural cotton" labels have found their way into no man's land: my laundry room.

Being the fashion-minded individuals they are, my sons have become quite fond of this latest vogue in clothing attire. Shirts, boldly emblazoned with logos of a well known soft drink, a miniscule little fellow astride a sporting pony, or the initials of a famous designer, are just a few of the creations I've noted. Trousers, board stiff, are, like the shirts, complete with a little washing instructions tag. It instructs the owner to "wash separately in cold water, hang to dry, and press with a warm iron." If each of these articles of clothing were washed separately, there would be a minimum of 27 mini loads per day, so I boldly intermingle them with each other. The pants are put on metal stretchers, one of my more useful garage sale items, which were popular a couple of decades ago, before perma-press. With several pair of pants suspended from the rafters, and the shirts on coat hangers swinging alongside them, all in a small windowless basement room, it looks like a sequel to "Halloween IV." The clothes dryer sits idly still, waiting for a load of damp towels to justify its existence.

I recall photos of primitive civilizations, seen in *National Geographic* magazine, with women washing clothing on the rocks of river banks, and I'm amazed at how far we've progressed as a society. We are so advanced in our intelligence quota that we pay outrageous prices to clothing manufacturers to outfit us in clothing that requires maximum upkeep. Thank goodness there is an iron on the market with a one size fits all handle. Anyone's hand will fit perfectly into it, even those of a teen-aged male wanting a specific shirt for a date.

The inspiration for this was my boss and iron loving friend, Most Reverend David R. Choby, Bishop of Nashville.

January 9, 1989

SHALL WE GATHER AT THE RIVER?
LIFE (BI) CYCLES

*I*t all started as soon as he discovered that wheels were round and they turned. For hours on end, our oldest son would sit, with toy car or truck, watching in utter fascination at the mechanism that propelled the vehicle forward or backward. He progressed from baby walker, which he preferred to push around empty, rather than sit in, to tricycle, to soap box derby car, to skateboard, to bicycle, to automobile. We bought band-aids by the gross to cover skinned elbows and knees, and got used to the tire pump on the front porch.

He wanted red tires for his purple bike one year, and his Grandmother saw to it that he got his wish. This was during the time when banana seats were the style, and he had a metallic silver one to add to the already colorful two-wheeler. Not noted for his agility, (a trait inherited from his dear old Mom), he had a fair number of mishaps, but what he lacked in grace, he more than compensated for in mechanical knowledge and skills. It was not unusual to see him completely disassemble his bike, or that of a friend, brother, or playmate, repair it, and save the defective or damaged parts for future use.

For a while, cars, school, and girls diverted his attention from his love of bicycles, but it returned in his adulthood to become an occupation, as well as a hobby, for him. He arrived at our front door one day last spring, wearing black stretch pants designed to fit a Ken doll, gloves with no fingers, a shirt that resembled a fluorescent pizza, and a short billed cap was pulled down, backwards, snugly over his head, He was in his sock feet, and was drinking from a small plastic bottle that looked as if it had just come from a hamster's cage. "Hi Mom. How do you like my racing bike?"

"Oh, it's nice, I guess. Where are your shoes? Surely you didn't ride all the distance from your house to ours without shoes", I said.

"No, no, I just took them off because they are special riding shoes, and it's not good to walk in them," he replied.

A college degree entitles one to such logic, I thought. Half a month's rent on riding shoes that can't be walked in must be beyond motherly comprehension.

"I want you and Dad to go bike riding. It'll be great exercise, and you'll love it."

"Do we have to wear shorts like yours?" I asked, mentally recalling the Hindenburg explosion.

"Only when you want to gain speed," he replied.

No need to worry about that, thank goodness.

In his typical thoughtful manner, this slim, considerate young man, restored my aging bicycle to it's better than new condition, and located a vintage Schwinn® bike for his father, which he completely refurbished. As our Christmas gift, he wanted us to get fit and healthy, and he had dedicated many hours of tedious, loving labor into that goal.

We got plenty of instructions before leaving on our maiden bike voyage. "Be sure to give hand signals, watch for oncoming traffic, use your brakes correctly, check your air in the tires, and get back home before dark. Oh, and don't tell anyone who you are, since you really aren't wearing correct bike clothing."

I thought my husband looked kinda nifty in his grey dress pants, and matching velour shirt, and my sweat band on the inside of my sun visor cap would surely be the envy of any biker we met along the way. The day after the ride, we re-discovered muscles that we thought had long since vanished, and aspirin was our constant companion. Our first destination was to the drugstore, and as soon as we're able to ride again, we'll make it to the chiropractor's office. Wonder if we can sell the bikes to get enough money to pay the doctor?

Over Budget-G.O.K.

The letters "G.O.K.", in my Grandmother's neat Palmer method script, appeared on every page of her monthly budget book. She was a real stickler for keeping an accurate and detailed record of expenses; a result, I'm sure, of her longstanding clerical position with the Internal Revenue Service. There could be dust bunnies under every piece of furniture in the house, a week's accumulation of dirty laundry, and dishes piled high in the sink, but her paperwork was meticulous, and took precedence over any of her household chores.

Not long after I mastered cursive writing, and labored to obtain my own distinctive signature, Grammie sat me down with a Palmer Method® penmanship workbook, and a stack of blank counter checks. She insisted that I practice my handwriting until it was legible and neat, and once I had passed her criteria, she showed me how to fill in the blank checks. Little did I realize she was preparing me for life with all those pages of cursive zeros and vertical lines.

The next lesson she had in store for me was making a budget, and using her's as an example, I dutifully headed up my imaginary household expenses. There was a column for rent, utilities, car payment, insurance, groceries, church donation, laundry and cleaning, telephone, and gasoline. I entered the "G.O.K." and asked her to explain it to me.

"Well, the 'G.O.K.' is for all the unexpected expenses that crop up each month, honey, and you'll have different amounts every time. Sometimes it's a small amount, and other months, it can be very large."

Her explanation seemed logical enough, and I entered $10 for my "G.O.K." I had a marvelous time writing my pretend checks and working with my make-believe budget, and when the time came for me to leave childhood behind, I was ready to take on the adult world, coached and cheered by Grammie, and armed with checkbook, pen, and ledger.

The early years of marriage found my budget floundering. We had to adjust the fixed expenses to encompass obstetrician visits, a washer and dryer, air conditioner, and maternity and baby clothes. My "G.O.K." ranged from $15 to $115 per month. Then we bought our house. Were we going to be able to afford that outlandish house payment of $88 every month? It seemed like a fortune at the time, and we spent many sleepless nights reworking our budget to cover all the anticipated expenses of homeowners and parents.

The pediatrician bill soon became a fixed expense, and just about the time I thought he'd get paid in full, along would come a virus, chickenpox, strep throat, ear infection, mumps, or an unexplained fever. Prescriptions were classified as "G.O.K", along with school photos, birthday presents for classmates' parties, and falls from bicycles and skateboards, which necessitated trips to hospital emergency rooms.

"G.O.K." covered new underwear in the fall, six winter boots, gloves and hats when the first snow fell, new football and basketball, baseball fees, and uniforms, plumbing leaks, parking tickets, paint for the house, shots for the dogs and cats, a water pump for the car, Santa Claus, Easter Bunny, Tooth Fairy, and Tupperware® purchases.

As time went by, the "G.O.K" went for prom flowers, tuxedo rentals, class rings, brake shoes, tennis shoes, home pack pizzas, orthodontist, income tax, increased car insurance premiums, appliance repairs, new tires, eyeglasses, school annuals, spring break trips, and a well-deserved vacation for two bedraggled parents.

The "G.O.K." expense will always be there, every month, ready to encompass sandboxes, swings, toys, and clothes for yet-to-be created grandchildren, and perhaps I'll have the opportunity someday to impart to another little girl the wisdom to anticipate what "God Only Knows."

Jℓanuary 9, 1990

WHERE HAVE ALL THE CHILDREN GONE?

The radio is set on the news station, and the television is tuned to CNN. Along with the rest of the world, on this dreary, misty winter day in January, I await results from the Geneva negotiations between U.S. Secretary of State James Baker and Iraqi Foreign Minister Tariq Aziz. I listen through the ears of a mother, rather than a political analyst or a military strategist. At this moment in history, I am neither Democrat nor Republican. I only long for the wish on our opened Christmas cards — Peace on earth ... Good will towards men.

I envision the faces of small, freckled face boys that used to ride bicycles on our street. Perhaps they might now be driving tanks across a desert. I remember seeing neighborhood children filling their plastic pails from a backyard sandbox, and I fear that some of them will have to see battle in a far-away country where sand covers everything, including the oil far below its surface.

When they were little, it was interesting to watch the boys pretending to be cops, robbers, cowboys, Indians, pirates, and soldiers. They would make tents in the back yard, and gather up flashlights, blankets, cans of Vienna sausages, crackers, Kool-Aid®, and "camp out." They were always so brave and tough, until a knee got scraped, or a splinter found its way into a dirty little finger, then it was time to head for the house, and get help from Mom. It was amazing what a needle, Band-Aid, soap and water, a hug, a lollipop, or a popsicle could cure.

We had our neighborhood bully. His name was Tommy, and he was big, strong, and meaner than a rattlesnake. All of the children loved to congregate at the "Honeycomb Hideout" — their secret clubhouse. None of the parents were supposed to know about it, but we all did. It was off limits to "gross" girls, but all the mongrel dogs were welcomed into the ramshackle haven. Tommy couldn't stand it any longer. He had no real friends, and he hated the fact that all the other children had such fun together. He staked his claim on the hideout, and forbade anyone from entering without his permission. The other boys, reluctant to tangle with him, decided that if they banned together, they could take possession and run him off. Tommy knew he was outnumbered, but his pride wouldn't allow him to admit defeat, and he refused to become their ally, so his solution was to tear down the hideout. He demolished it one dark night, reducing what had once been a lively gathering place to a pile of scrap lumber and rusty nails. If he couldn't have it all to his miserable self, nobody else would enjoy it either.

As with Tommy's line of reasoning, the war clouds continue to gather over the Persian Gulf. Learned men continue to debate the reasons, resolutions, military strategies, and political protocol. Deadlines are set, ultimatums are issued, and families worry and pray for their husbands, wives, sons, daughters, fathers, mothers, sweethearts, sisters, brothers, aunts, uncles, cousins, or friends who will be on the battlefields. Each military person is some mother's child, whatever their nationality.

There will be no Mammas to run to if battle breaks out. No band-aids, lollipops, or popsicles to soothe away the pain, and no reassuring hugs to send them back to their tents.

Charles Osgood summed up the tense situation well: "God created the Persian Gulf; Man created the Persian Gulf crisis."

May 15, 1991

JUST WHEN YOU THINK
THEY'VE FLOWN THE NEST

They were addressed, stamped, and ready to mail. The formally engraved invitations, tucked inside the second double envelope, read, "The President, Faculty, and Graduating Class announce Commencement Exercises." There were two cards enclosed, one with the date, time, and location of the ceremony, and the other engraved with the, hopefully familiar to the recipients, name of our college graduate.

Having lived away from home for the number of years it required him to earn this coveted sheepskin, his commencement also heralded the move back home. He had assured us that he had either sold, given away, trashed, abandoned, recycled, or bribed someone to take, most of his well-used apartment furniture. It had been functional, and consisted mainly of early attic furnishings from family members, mixed in with a bit of Salvation Army bargains. Definitely not the decor that constituted a photo layout in Southern Living.

"I only have my personal stuff left to move home."

After he unloaded his clothes, and some linens from his small, foreign, four door sedan, I was pleasantly relieved to see that it all fit into his old room. His former room had been reduced, significantly, in size when I finally got my long awaited walk-in closet last summer. He correctly equates the present size of his livable space with that of a small ship's cabin. When he asked to borrow the pickup truck, to haul another load home, I should have suspected that his stuff was going to require a bit more storage space.

Two days, and three truck loads later, the garage door wouldn't close, the riding mower was covered by boxes of textbooks, his twin bed was sagging from the weight of stacked boxes, the washer was in a constant spin cycle, and there were damp cotton sweatshirts hanging from every rafter of the basement laundry room. His pots, pans, dishes, and party memorabilia were on top of the chest freezer, his compact disk and tape collection had infiltrated our Jackie

Gleason/ Vicki Carr record storage cabinet, and the "walk-in" closet wasn't. His bicycle was on the porch, and the attic storage reached overload capacity in a few hours. Somehow, however, he had managed to empty his campus apartment, and relocate all his worldly goods among our other trash and treasures.

His dog, who had grown fat, depressed, listless, and lazy while his master was away pursuing an education, was again chasing Frisbees, and smiling contentedly. He was clearly delighted to have some activity around the house once more. The only thing the dog and I didn't have in common was fleas, and the fact that I refused to retrieve the Frisbee.

After a hectic week of moving, final exams, and graduation preparations, our youngest son was about to receive his diploma. From our viewing point, very high in the auditorium, the entire graduating class resembled an ant colony.

There were over a thousand graduates, marching in the largest class in the history of his alma mater, but like a mother seal, on a crowded beach of seemingly identical pups, I spotted him among the capped and gowned masses.

"Look, there he is, get his picture," I urged loudly to my husband.

"Where? How on earth can you spot him from up here?"

"Right there. See that post with the yellow marks? Well, just look to the left of it a smidgen, count four to the right, go eight rows down, and ... oh, look he's rubbing his ear. Don't you see him?"

He finally zeroed in on him when his turn came to walk up and receive his diploma, and captured the moment on video, before he disappeared into the sea of tasseled mortar boards.

College is over, at last, and if we can find the typewriter, the fine art of writing resumes and scouring the want ads begins once more.

July 6, 1992

HOME'S TRUE HEART
IS THE DINING ROOM TABLE

A conference table is an impressive, and vitally important, piece of furniture in the board room of successful businesses. It is large enough to accommodate all involved members of a firm, yet small enough to encourage conversation and the feeling of unity. Usually flanked by plush, comfortable chairs that are designed to put their occupants at ease, it becomes the site of most major corporate discussions and decisions.

Like the conference table, a family dining table becomes the gathering spot for household members. They dash by, barely stopping long enough to wolf down a bowl of cereal, a glass of juice, or a travel mug of coffee to go, on rushed morning departures. If anyone is around at lunchtime, it's most often to pick up a sandwich or a quick snack as they scatter in various directions. Supper, the traditional meal when families used to sit down together for a relaxing meal, has become a progressive affair, where food portions are often set aside to microwave, as various schedules permit solitary dining.

Whether modern, traditional, antique, or flea market find, the style of table is relatively unimportant. It might be chrome, wood, glass, or even cardboard, and can be located in the kitchen, den, dining room, or porch. Round, square, oblong, or hexagon, they can be as small as a coffee table or large enough to accommodate a banquet. The composition, placement, shape, and sizes are as varied as the individuals that utilize them.

In a rented apartment, plans for a first home are spread out on the table, and a budget is carefully planned to allow enough cash flow for the anticipated monthly house note. If a baby arrives, the table becomes the site of the infant's bath, and a high chair gets scooted up to the edge. Although candles increase in number on birthday cakes, only the table remains unchanged, except for a few scratches, by the years. As the family expands, so does the table, with the addition of leaves and extensions. Holiday dinners get piled high atop the table, and the family shares many memorable meals as they exchange stories and laughter.

The daily paper is spread out on the table; national and local news is eagerly read and discussed.

"Did you see where Mr. Brown's sister died last night?"

"Look at this terrific sale going on at the mall."

"I still can't decide who to vote for in this election."

"Who cut out the other side of the recipe for cheeseless cheesecake?"

"Wow, look at the ad on this car, Dad."

"Mom, can we go to this movie?"

"How about going to the ball game tomorrow with me?"

"Save the classified job ads for me."

"Where did they hide the crossword puzzle this time?"

When television is into re-runs, and everyone gets restless, the table becomes the site of a (hopefully) friendly card game, chess, checkers, Monopoly, or other board game. The hours pass quickly as everyone gets involved, and the desire to emerge as winner becomes very important to some.

Grocery lists are composed, coloring book and crayon masterpieces are painstakingly created, graduation and wedding invitations are addressed, thank you notes are laboriously printed under Mom's watchful eye. Christmas card lists are updated and utilized, letters are written to friends and family separated by distance, and household insomniacs sit alone, in the wee hours of the morning, playing solitaire while seated at the table.

Unexpected guests drop in, and conversation flows around the table as freely as the steaming cups of coffee or tea. It seems to be the logical spot where school books and mail are dropped off, homework gets done, notes are left, rules are reinforced, tears are spilled, laughter is shared, and plans are made for changes. Much more than a piece of furniture where empty tummies get filled, it is the center of a household, a place to exchange feelings, ideas, secrets, and dreams.

I wonder if a tuna casserole would look out of place on a conference table?

August 23, 2015

SOMEWHERE OVER THE RAINBOW

Despite my best attempts to sleep late in my retirement, the years of early rising to prepare for a work day have left their mark on my internal alarm clock. I awaken each day before my spouse, and have found that this is my time alone to reflect, pray, and organize the hours ahead. The house is quiet, with only the barely audible sound of the refrigerator motor. There are no phone calls or door bells to interrupt my thoughts, and the radio and television are silent.

For a long time, I fought getting up from the comfort of my bed, but the harder I fought it, the more my mind would gallop off into 20 different directions. I would do laundry, make grocery lists, catch up on correspondence, jot down ideas for future columns, clip coupons, or play solitaire. Then one day, I figured out that I was waking up early for a reason. Maybe God was trying to get my attention while there were no other distractions competing with Him for my undivided attention. He was trying to show me the world around me.

The first time I tried sitting perfectly still and just living in the moment. I felt guilty for being idle. There were no booming voices speaking directly to me from heaven, and I fidgeted while sitting all alone in my living room. It gave me the sensation that I was waiting for company to arrive. I only lasted about 10 minutes, and then moved on to the kitchen to find something more productive to do.

Soon I was looking forward to my early morning routine. It seemed to set the tempo for the remainder of my day. Different people would come to mind as my brain took off on its own, and I realized that they might need some prayers, so I acted upon those urgings. When the weather permitted, I found that being outside in the morning was a thing of beauty to behold and experience. Even the rain seemed to be giving me the knowledge that it was providing for growth and necessary moisture for the soil, and I prayed that some of it would find its way to the fire ravaged states of California and Washington.

One rainy overcast morning I was outside, dry and shielded by our patio cover. It was gray and gloomy with not a sign of sunshine anywhere. I was preparing to go back inside when something caught my attention. The soft whirring sound alerted me to the fact that a visitor was close at hand. A tiny hummingbird darted towards the hanging feeder, intent on beating its companions to breakfast. As she sipped the nectar from the plastic flowers on the feeder, two others swooped in on her, and the squeaks and territorial battle commenced. Each one would grab a quick snack and then dash off quickly, only to return over and over again. Darting back and forth like winged bullets, they seemed to be in perpetual motion. I marveled at their tenacity and ability to hover in the air above their feeder.

While watching this fascinating display of nature, I caught a glimpse of something colorful in the sky. A brilliant rainbow arched through the grey clouds overhead. The vivid red, blue, yellow, green, and purple bands formed a perfect semi-circle that lasted about 10 minutes before it gradually faded. Unlikely visions of a happy little mythical leprechaun, dancing a jig beside a huge pot of gold at the end of the rainbow, failed to diminish the beauty of the colorful phenomena.

There is a lengthy, technical explanation for the cause and effect of rainbows, involving the process of refraction or the bending of light. However, I chose to disregard all of that and just accept it for the message it seemed to bring to me. "After the rain comes the rainbow" seemed to be screaming at me loud and clear. "I will set my bow in the clouds, and it shall be the sign of a covenant between me, and between the earth." (Genesis 9:13)

I shall continue to try to sleep a bit later each morning, but then I realize how much I would miss in the world around me.

FINAL SUNSETS

Chapter

REQUIEM FOR MY UNCLE

"And I give unto them eternal life, and they shall never perish." (John 10:28). To the heart of anyone who has been touched by the loss of a loved one, there is a great deal of comfort to be found in this passage from the Bible.

My family has again sought solace for the ache of death's pain, as we were touched by this necessary, but painful element of life.

My uncle, although in his mid-seventies and still actively working in our family owned business, was abruptly called from this life as he was a spectator to his favorite sporting event. He had no forewarning, no time to prepare for the journey that each of us must someday take. His untimely passing reminds us of our own immortality, and we mourn not only our sense of loss for his presence in our midst, but for the fact that life is but a temporary thing.

His nature was brusque, even abrasive at times. He had the uncanny ability to dominate almost every situation, and his blustery, gruff exterior camouflaged the tenderness he was afraid to expose, but was nonetheless manifested in countless ways.

He spurned fashion, and stubbornly clung to his old, comfortable, dated wardrobe. With a cap sitting jauntily sideways on his head and his well worn trousers far below his paunchy waist, he presented an almost comical appearance. But woe to those who dared to smile at this genuine individualist.

I remember vividly a day that he took me to school. When I told him I needed lunch money, he gave me a veritable treasure for a little girl of 5: a whole paper folding dollar. I was so ecstatic over my newfound prosperity. I impulsively hugged the neck of my bachelor uncle and embarrassed both of us.

He remained single until mid-life, and after his marriage, his home became the scene for many happy family gatherings, among them the wedding rehearsal dinner for my husband and me. There were many Christmases, with all the nieces and nephews eagerly tearing into brightly wrapped gifts, and abundant food heaped onto appetizing tables. Everyone was welcomed warmly, and it was always a pleasure to be a guest of his.

The news of his unexpected demise has had a profound effect on those of us he has left behind to grieve. There are unspoken words within the confines of each heart, conversations we wish we had initiated with him. Now we must bid farewell to a part of every one of us, and it is a painful process.

We unite in our sorrow, as a family should, sharing the burden of bereavement. The warm and caring condolences of our friends sustain us, alleviating some of our suffering, and reaffirm our faith in our fellow man. Although some are at a loss for words, these mourners pay a fitting and lasting tribute to his memory by their physical presence among us.

His human imperfections and faults are forgotten, and we focus on the positive aspects of his life, the good deeds he performed for others, and we pray that the Lord he always loved and respected will do the same.

Until we meet again in our eternal home, rest in peace, Uncle Buddy, and may perpetual light ever shine upon your soul.

September 14, 1988

UNFADED MEMORIES

She can't understand why things are so darned expensive. Why, even the Sunday paper costs over a dollar, and a bottle of Coca-Cola® is 50 cents in the machine down in the laundry room. Seems as though the whole world has gone mad in pricing things right out of reach of older folks living on a fixed income, and besides that, the doctors poke their head in, say hello to you, after you sat and waited half the live-long afternoon in that drafty waiting room, and send you a bill that almost causes a heart attack.

She keeps the heat on year round in the tiny apartment, and sits in front of the television from sunup to sundown pausing only to use the bathroom, to fix a bite to eat, or to check the mailbox for a welcome letter from a friend or relation, but there is only more junk mail and dreaded bills. Her vision is poor, and her hearing worse, so she can't do the needlework that used to occupy her hands, mind, and time. Her link to the outside world, the telephone, has now become more a source of aggravation than the pleasure that it once was. She asks those people to quit calling her about insurance and credit cards, but they just keep right on talking until she hangs up.

She drags out the tattered box of old photographs and letters, and begins to reminisce about the people and events that these things call to mind. There's the snapshot that she and her big brother had posed for, on the front of Grandma's porch, she in her white cotton stockings and freshly laundered dress that Mamma had made for her, and Brother, hair slicked down, knickers that he longed to grow out of, and his shoes reflecting much spit and polish, side by side, fingers of their hands intertwined. How she had adored this big brother of hers! She grasped another photo in her arthritic fingers, and smiled at the image of Brother in his World War I uniform, so handsome, tall, and dashing. Mamma and Papa had prayed so hard for him while he was overseas, and she didn't think she'd ever see him alive again. The good Lord had heard their pleas, however, and he had returned safely to marry, and raise a family. She never had any children of her own, so her nephews and niece became her surrogates, and she doted on them.

She looked now at a picture of herself and her husband, and recalled the day that they had gone on a family picnic in the country, and how she had to persuade him to pose for the photograph. He was self-conscious about having his picture taken, but once she used her feminine wiles on him, he could deny her nothing, so he relented. Although he couldn't manage to smile for the camera, and looked rather unhappy, she displayed a toothsome grin to the unknown photographer's box camera.

The memories were clear in her mind, and the sight of those loved ones gave her great comfort and pleasure. She recalled, with a fond smile, the day she first drove an automobile. Papa was astonished, Mama was aghast, Brother beamed at her daring, and her poor husband shook with fear, in the seat beside her, as she motored around the cobblestone streets, waving to all who saw her. If she could only have a car now, she could still manage to go where she wanted. She couldn't understand why they had decided that she wasn't capable of controlling an automobile. Those accidents were not her fault, and the car didn't look all that bad with the dents in the fenders. The insurance people kept sending her bigger and bigger bills though, and the brakes finally gave way on the faded blue vintage car. She was now at the mercy of whoever was kind enough to do her shopping, errands, or take her to her increasingly frequent physicians' appointments.

As she sat in the reclining rocking chair, fatigue and weakness caused her to doze off. There they were again; Mama, Papa, Brother, her precious husband, niece, nephews, aunts, uncles, cousins, friends, and neighbors, all talking to her, sharing confidences, exchanging gossip, and surrounding her with their love. She opened her bright blue eyes, and after a few moments, stared around the empty room to look for them. All that remained, however, was the large, yellowed box of mementos on the coffee table.

April 21, 1989

AND I REMEMBER MAMMA

She was not like all the other mothers. She was younger, livelier, more outgoing, and she loved to laugh. During my teen years, when, I'm now certain she would have liked to disown me, her laughter embarrassed me, for it was loud, hearty, and genuine. I wanted her to be quieter, more reserved, dignified and much less outspoken and opinionated than she was. I was forever trying, in vain, to get her to dress differently, change her hairstyle, talk softer, and be more punctual. It didn't matter where she went, she was always 30 minutes late, minimum, and I longed for the day that I could get my driver's license, and be independent of her habitual tardiness.

A fabulous cook, she never measured anything, and I found it impossible to duplicate even one of her many recipes. Her biscuits, rather than being light, tall and fluffy, were large, flat, laden with shortening, and utterly divine. My brother and I fought over the day old ones, knowing how good they were, split and toasted. Though Irish by heritage, as well as in temperament, she learned to make authentic Italian meatballs and sauce from her mother-in-law, my paternal grandmother, and this specialty of hers became legendary among friends, family, and my prospective suitors. I begged her not to betray my inability to cook, and successfully convinced one very important fellow that I could cook just like my mamma.

I hated for people to comment that "You look just like your mother," I saw no resemblance between the two of us and was mystified when people always marveled at the likeness between us. She had fair skin, that freckled easily, while mine was a drab olive color. Her eyes were vivid blue, in direct contrast to my dark brown ones, and her prematurely grey hair had never been as dark as mine. She was, in my eyes, beautiful, and I knew in my heart that I was no match for her looks.

We never saw eye to eye on anything. Our taste in clothes, furniture, music, and household decor were exactly opposite. Her formal living room, furnished in her prized antiques, was dubbed the "Hermitage," and was off limits to just about everyone but her bridge club. Mine, on the other hand, was all the name "living" implied, much to my chagrin and her displeasure. She chastised me for my lack of neatness, and I urged her to become more relaxed in her fastidious housekeeping. So different, yet so alike in moods and thoughts that if one day passed without hearing from one another, panic set in. As I grew older, I was delighted to discover that Mamma acquired much more sense.

An adoring grandmother to the three grandsons that her well loved son-in-law and I produced, she found it easier to lavish gifts and treats on them, rather than words of praise. I knew that the pride and love she had for them was not easy for her to express verbally, and the facade of good natured bantering she exchanged with them amused and amazed them.

Each Friday, after her weekly hair appointment, she would load up grocery sacks with all the treats they loved, and headed for our front door with the bulging bags of ice cream sandwiches, hard salami, cream filled cookies, real Cokes, candy, and assorted favorite cheeses. It was difficult to determine who derived the most pleasure from the treats; she, in watching the boys pig out, or they, eagerly stuffing their tummies.

Mamma never backed away from a fight in her entire life, and she usually came out the winner. Her final foe, however, proved to be a much too powerful adversary for her. The disease that broke her in body and spirit claimed her before she reached the age of 60, taking my very best friend from my life.

"You're so much like your mother," someone commented recently.

"Thank you so much. My Mamma was quite some lady," I replied truthfully.

November 22, 1993

I'll Remember John Kennedy .... And Weep

Thirty years ago they shot our President.

"They, or he?"

Oh, oh, here comes yet another theory on the assassination. Wrong. Having read several books, seeing "JFK," and watching all the television specials about John Kennedy, I, like so many others, still cannot be positive about the motives, plots, or the killers. Did Lee Harvey Oswald act alone, or did he have accomplices? Was there only one gunman firing three shots, or three different guns, each fired from separate locations, by strategically placed individuals? Did the bullets come from the Texas Book Depository, or the grassy knoll, or perhaps, both? Was it a conspiracy masterminded by the Mafia, or maybe Castro? Was his body switched before burial? Perhaps the truth will never be known, or at least not in my lifetime.

It is strange to be a witness to history. Like an aged Civil War widow who vividly recalls the bloody battle waged in her Daddy's cornfield, the events of that terrible day are engraved forever in my memory. On November 22, 1963, almost every American remembers where they were, and what they were doing when the first news hit. I was 23 years old, younger than any of my children are now. My life centered around the never ending needs of our 2-year-old son, and I was three months pregnant with his yet to be born brother. Politically ignorant, I was nonetheless enchanted with the Camelot era in Washington, and felt that 46-year-old Jack Kennedy was a good leader of our nation. My grandmother thought he was the greatest thing since sliced bread, and she adored the entire Kennedy clan. To her Irish Catholic way of thinking, he personified American royalty, and she visibly bristled if anyone dared to speak unfavorably about them in her presence. Had she lived to hear the stories of his alleged marital indiscretions now, I'm certain she would have never believed a single word, and most certainly she would have chastised those who told about them.

Although she wore a "pillbox" on her well coiffed hairdo, and I kept my

215

"pill box" in the medicine cabinet, I empathized with Jackie Kennedy when she lost little Patrick Bouvier. Having also lost a son at birth, I sympathized with the pain that she and the President must have felt, and for the first and only time in my life, I sent a note of heartfelt sympathy to the White House. That made them human to me, and I prayed for their sadness. They, like us, had small children, and we identified with their family unit.

The very first Presidential ballot on which I was old enough to cast my vote had his name on it. The first time I stayed up all night to watch the outcome of election returns was the year he was elected to become the 35th president of the United States. We went to Vanderbilt Stadium when he spoke in Nashville, and still have the home movies that my husband was tenacious enough to film.

Until Kennedy became president, I never related to that office, but, in 1961, as I entered adulthood, I succumbed to the charisma of our handsome leader.

At work on November 22, 1963, someone notified me to turn on the radio. "The President has been shot."

I turned the radio up louder, thinking that I had not heard the newscaster correctly.

"President Kennedy was shot just a short while ago, as his motorcade traveled through Dealey Plaza in Dallas, Texas. No immediate word on his condition is available."

No longer able to concentrate on the work piled on the desk in front of me, I was unable to move away from the radio, as continued updates were broadcast. There was one tiny window in my office, and from it, if I stood on a chair, there was a clear view of the Tennessee State Capitol building. Before I heard the tragic fate of the President, I saw the flag lower over the Capitol, and I cried as if I had lost a close member of my family. I cried for his family, my family, the nation, and the entire world. I cried during the days that followed, as I watched his funeral entourage on TV, and I cried to think that anyone could do such a heinous deed.

Yes, I remember that day all too well, and when my grandchildren read about John Kennedy's assassination in their history books, I shall weep anew as I tell them I saw it.

March 16, 1994

AUNT MYRT RACKED UP PLENTY
OF TROPHIES IN NINETY-SEVEN YEARS

The wooden cross stood, draped in purple, adorned with a crown of thorns. In its stark simplicity, the message of Jesus' crucifixion was compelling and powerful. As the Mass continued, I meditated on the suffering and death of Christ. The communion hymn began; "On a hill far away stood an old rugged cross."

How many times I had heard another congregation sing those words. As a child, I loved to go to church with my great aunt, and listen to her singing loudly and sincerely. My mother gave her a small electric organ for Christmas one year, and she would sit down, and sing "The Old Rugged Cross" over and over, without ever tiring or losing her enthusiasm. As she made dumplings, fried chicken, or stirred cornbread batter, she would hum the tune and cheerfully praise heaven from her kitchen. Dinner was the meal at mid-day, and the pots of home cooked vegetables were left on the gas stove after everyone ate their fill, to be eaten again at supper time.

Aunt Myrt, my maternal grandfather's younger, and only, sister was spoiled by her parents, adored by her big brother, and used to getting her own way. When she was 14, one of Nanny and Paw-Paw's boarders from the Monroe Harding Home found Myrtle to be everything he wanted in a wife. So, on her 15th birthday, June 29, 1912, in her parents' parlor, Myrtle Elizabeth Hurt married Jesse Gordon Peak.

Jesse spoiled her too. How could he help but give in to any whim of hers, once she looked at him with those breathtakingly beautiful blue eyes? They were a brilliant penetrating clear blue, the color of sky, with the twinkle of diamonds. They held deep within them laughter, innocence, and a determined spirit.

She was a tall woman, who carried her well corseted self proudly. It never seemed to bother her, or Uncle Jesse, that he was only 4'8", while she towered over him by almost a foot. He was a bookkeeper for the grainery, and she was a home based hairdresser, who later sold cleaning products and brushes at home parties. She wanted to drive an automobile, and persisted until she mastered the complicated machine that Jesse bought for her. He was too short to reach the gas and brake pedals, so she became the permanent designated driver.

As the years passed, it became painfully evident that parenthood was not going to be theirs, but with lots of love to give, they showered all their attentions on nieces, nephews, and cousins. "Brother's" daughter, Martha, became the daughter they always wanted. Blessed with Myrtle's eyes, she loved them both unconditionally. Myrtle would take her, and her two younger brothers, to Centennial Park to feed the ducks, and she sewed bonnets and frilly dresses for her on the treadle sewing machine.

After Martha married, they were elated when she brought them a new baby girl to love. She had straight black hair, a fat little round face, and her eyes were dark brown rather than blue. Aunt Myrt spent hours coaxing my straight locks around metal curlers, and bribed me with magazines to sit under her formidable looking hair dryer. I was subjected to a torturous and very smelly permanent three times each year, with resulting frizz that made me look like Roseann Roseanna Danna. She gave me new nylon underwear from prestigious Cain Sloan's department store every Christmas, and she would drag me with her as she traveled all around the state, selling her cleaning products and brushes. She was a natural salesperson, demonstrating the amazing powers of her products, while keeping the rural female audiences entertained with her games and prizes.

For their 50th wedding anniversary, we had a quiet celebration and a cake with a golden bell. Four years later Uncle Jesse, the small man with such a big heart, passed away, leaving Myrtle to mourn. She was a part of every family holiday celebration, contributing Nanny's famous buttermilk pies as a favorite dessert choice. Every morning she'd put on one of her starched housedresses and nylon hose, sweep off the front sidewalk, cook bacon or sausage with eggs, coffee and canned buttered biscuits. She never ate a tossed salad, fresh seafood, or any meat that wasn't fried and covered with gravy. She used lard in her pie crust, and held up her stockings with round elastic garters, or by knotting them tightly just above her knees.

She outlived most of her relatives and friends, and found herself struggling with remote controlled televisions, microwave ovens, automated banking machines, and panty hose. She lived her almost 97 years without ever taking a plane or boat trip, and could count the movies she had seen in a theater on one hand. As her physical limitations increased, and her short term memory diminished, she moved from house to retirement apartment, and, finally, to a nursing home. She read her Bible daily, and remained always true to the teachings of her faith. This Easter season, Aunt Myrt has "at last her trophies lay down," and exchanged her old rugged cross for a crown in heaven, where the angels clamor for a piece of her legendary buttermilk pie.

March 1, 2009

LITTLE WOMAN WITH A BIG HEART

*S*he graduated from high school in 1936. Seven years later, when she married her grammar school sweetheart, they had a big wedding that not only united them as husband and wife for 65 years, but connected her forever to his entire family. My uncle Jim was the third of four children of my grandparents. They were a close knit Italian family, and when Frances married Jim, she probably hadn't a clue that she was taking on his entire clan. She started their married life as an Air Force wife in Midland, Texas, where their first son was born in a military hospital. They returned to Nashville three years later where two more sons were born, followed by the birth of their youngest, a little girl. She was not only a full-time wife, mother, and homemaker, a loving daughter to her own parents, but she was a devoted daughter-in-law, sister-in-law, and aunt to all of the children, whether related to her by blood or by marriage.

There were nine grandchildren on our side of the family, and Aunt Frances played an important role in each of our lives. When she was a young bride, she and my mother were taught by Grandma to make Italian meatballs and "gravy." At Christmas, they joined my Godmother, and their other sister-in-law, in one of the grand traditions of our family: the ravioli construction project and the "Cucchidati and Biscotti bakeoff." All of the family gathered each December 25, originally at Grandma and Papa's house, to feast on the fantastic secret recipe ravioli and cookies that had originated in Sicily. As the family grew, and after Grandpa passed away on Easter Sunday, 1952, the annual Christmas gathering continued, but rotated between the homes of the three sons each year. I still marvel to think of the preparation and planning that went into hosting more than 50 relatives on Christmas Day, but I'm sure that all of my cousins and my daddy would agree that this is one of the fondest memories we all will forever share. Everyone would always head home in the evening with leftover ravioli, a tin of the cucchidati and biscotti, and a bank envelope with cash from Grandma.

Aunt Frances was a diminutive lady, but boy, could she work circles around anyone! She was constantly in motion, and was second to none in her ability to sew, cook, and create all sorts of interesting craft projects. She was a collector, and anyone who has ever been to her home could attest to the fact that she probably had more refrigerator magnets, stuffed animals, seasonal decorations, and knick knacks than anyone on this planet. But she also collected the respect and admiration of those who knew her. She worked tirelessly on countless school projects for her children, for the nuns who taught her children in school, and was always willing to take on anyone or anything that came her way. She was tenacious and fiercely protective of those she loved. Every holiday, their home on was extensively decorated both inside and out.

All little girls like to play dress-up, and I was no exception. However, while others clunked around in their mother's oversized high heels, I was the envy of all, because thanks to Aunt Frances' tiny hand me down shoes, my high heels fit me perfectly! She made doll beds from wooden spools, and Cinderella coaches from styrofoam. She was one of those talented people who could take popsicle sticks and transform them into a sled for a Santa doll.

With the same passion she utilized to create decorations, she poured her boundless energy into parenting her three sons and only daughter. She was a devoted mother, an extremely proud grandmother, and the epitome of the word "great-grandmother." It was Aunt Frances who I turned to when I wanted purple velvet hats and muffs for my winter wedding attendants, and it was she who covered the baby bassinet in pale yellow and mint green for our anticipated first baby. She also gave me some of the best advice any new mother could ever get: "Run the vacuum cleaner and turn on the radio when you bring that baby home from the hospital. Don't go tip-toeing around the house all day ... When your boys grow taller than you, swat 'em with a broom when they misbehave." It worked so well, my children could sleep through an earthquake, and ran quickly for cover whenever I attempted to sweep the kitchen.

When my uncle died, her mind could not bear to accept a life without him, so it took her to a place that removed her from reality and grief. She has left all of her collections behind now, and gone on to join her parents, brothers and sister, cherished aunts, all the many deceased members of our family, and her beloved husband and youngest son.

At her funeral the priest noted that her metal casket would have been the perfect place to attach her prized magnets. She would have loved that creative touch.

January 26, 2015

Death Of Classmate Causes Regrets

Our high school graduation class was small; just 25 girls at a private Catholic academy. Although small in number, we were diverse in appearance, talents, and personalities. Our uniforms were identical in various sizes, but that was where our similarities ceased. As teenagers in the '50's, we enjoyed our music, dancing, dating, and slumber parties, and most of us just tolerated school. We didn't realize at the time how fortunate we were. The nuns that taught us in class re-enforced the ideals and principles that our parents had instilled in us from the cradle. We were told that we represented our school, our families, and our faith whenever we appeared in public, and we all knew that we had better act like ladies or deal with dire consequences. Our teachers were surely the originators of zero tolerance. One misstep and it was all over. If you messed up and got into trouble at school, you got doubly disciplined when your parents heard about it.

Among the class members, some were more popular than others, some were shy, and others outgoing. We were blondes, brunettes, and a feisty redhead, predominantly sporting the ponytailed fashion of our day, but with a few pixie cuts and short hair interspersed. In this pre-contact lens era, some wore glasses while I was the lone "metal mouth" who needed braces, much to my disdain. Our homes were in various parts of the city, and some traveled a great distance to school. A few lucky ones got their own cars when we turned 16, while the rest of us rode the bus, bummed a ride, walked, or depended on our parents to drive us to and from weekday classes.

After we graduated and went our separate ways, promising to stay in touch with one another, we took different paths in life. While a few married and started families, one entered the convent, others went to work full time, and college life beckoned several of us. Career opportunities for women were not as available or accessible as they are now, consequently not all who started college remained to graduate.

Among our group, there was one quiet, studious girl who made excellent grades and never caused any trouble. She was short in stature, with long naturally curly hair that I envied. Never one to call attention to herself, she obeyed all the rules, and if she ever missed one day of school, I cannot recall when it might have been. If they had given a perfect attendance award, she surely would have gotten it.

The years passed. We each got involved in our own hectic lives of families, schedules, jobs, housekeeping, and the fast pace of daily life. When we had class reunions, we would vow to never let another year pass without contacting one another, but somehow we would all go back into our own routines, and wonder aloud where the time went when we next gathered.

A couple of years ago, this quiet studious girl came once more to our reunion and shared with us that she was battling cancer. We were concerned about her and offered her our support, love, and prayers. I compiled an updated contact list for everyone, and e-mailed her from time to time to see how she was getting along. Rounds of radiation, chemotherapy and treatment for the cancer took its toll on her physically.

Each day, as I remembered her in my prayers, I would tell myself that I would pick up the phone and give her a call just to see how she was. My good intentions never materialized, and an e-mail to her just before this Christmas went unanswered. Thanks to modern communication methods, I googled her and was shocked when her out-of-state obituary came up. She had died in the summer, survived by her husband, four children, and three grandchildren. Tears of sorrow and regret cannot erase the terrible guilt I feel for not making the extra effort to reach out to Loretta during her final struggle. My prayer is that she somehow knew how important she was and what an inspiration she was by her gentle and unassuming manner.

"Priorities"
Mary Margaret Lambert

The sad news came just the other day
That a dear old friend had passed away.
I'd been meaning to visit, or perhaps just call,
But I've been so busy with the kids and all.
Now as I prepare to pay my final respects,
I feel sad inside, and awfully vexed
Because of unspoken words I shall now never speak,
And I feel tears of remorse steam down my cheek.
Why didn't I just say "I love you my friend"
Before this precious life came to an end?

February 1, 2010

EXPIRATION DATES

*L*ike many other people who are trying to find ways of saving money wherever I can, I clip coupons. It is not a job I particularly relish, but when I see the amount of savings on my grocery receipt, it does seem like using them pays off. Now, I am not one of those women you read about who purchases $150 worth of groceries for $1.29. Those overzealous ladies are in a different league from me. They belong to coupon clubs, and when they go shopping, they take huge briefcases filled with their coupons, not a small wallet size cardboard folder like the one I use. I am just the garden variety coupon clipper who sits down once a week with the inserts from the Sunday paper, and clips only the coupons that I know I will use for products I normally buy. The biggest drawback for me is the dreaded expiration dates that are printed on each and every one. I estimate that half of the coupons I accumulate will expire before I have the chance to redeem them, so they end up in the recycle bin without ever getting used.

It seems that everything has an expiration date: from makeup to drivers' licenses, there is a month, day and year stamped on the top, side or bottom of nearly everything in our house. I grabbed some sinus headache medicine from the bathroom cabinet last week, and was so happy to find it that I swallowed two of the tablets before I checked the expiration date on the package. It went out of date two years ago. Did that mean that it was no longer going to be effective? Was I going to experience some weird symptoms that would send me searching frantically for the phone number of poison control? Would my headache grow worse as a result of ingesting the outdated meds? A thousand and one unanswered questions swirled about in my already throbbing head, but within an hour, my pain had subsided, and I felt none the worse for my mistake.

An encouraging article from *Pyschopharmacology Today* advises, "Most of what is known about drug expiration dates comes from a study conducted by the Food and Drug Administration at the request of the military. With a large and expensive stockpile of drugs, the military faced tossing out and replacing its drugs every few years. What they found from the study is 90 percent of more than 100 drugs, both prescription and over-the-counter, were perfectly good to use even 15 years after the expiration date." Luckily, I saved the rest of that outdated package of sinus meds, because according to this information, I'm good until 2023.

I did a little research the following day on expiration dates and their meaning and learned, much to my surprise, that "dating is not federally required, except for infant formula and baby food. States have varying laws. Most states require that milk and other perishables be sold before the expiration date." I must admit that I have consumed yogurt that is past its prime by a couple of weeks, only to live and suffer no adverse effects, and I have also found that cheese, as long as it doesn't have green, fuzzy stuff growing on it, seems to be perfectly palatable. In checking the milk in the refrigerator, if the date is past, I just rely on my nose to let me know if it's ok to pour over my cereal. I do check the dates on everything I buy at the stores, and if the milk only has a couple of days before it goes out of date, I dig around for a much younger container.

It was interesting to note that deodorant doesn't expire for two years and a bar of soap is good for up to three years. Hopefully, no one I come in contact with will take that long to use either of these essential toiletry items. There is one particular brewery that stamps its product with a "born on" date, and it is recommended that it should be consumed within four months of that date. This has never been an issue at our house.

The wise and prudent thing to do, I suppose, would be to promptly use and enjoy everything before it reaches its expiration date. This is true for food, medications, cosmetics, coupons and for ourselves. Our expiration dates are not known, but it's important to make the most of every day before they run out.

April 8, 2005

MOURNING DOVES BRING COMFORT DURING TRAGEDY

*E*very morning, as I walked out of our house and onto the patio, I was somewhat startled by a pair of birds who would take off and fly directly in front of me.

Perched on the wall, they watched me intently, and acted as though I was intruding into their private space. But they were the visitors and, not wanting to appear inhospitable, I just bid them a good morning and left them on their own while I was at work. It didn't occur to me that they were checking out the neighborhood and planning to take up residence with us.

In the early morning hours, while daylight was still struggling to appear, I would hear a faint, mournful cooing sound outside our bedroom window, and I realized that our visiting birds were doves. They were grayish brown in color and were always together, so we assumed they were a couple. As with all things in our lives, from cars and houses to children, we named her "Cooey" and he was "Mr. Gray."

It didn't take long to figure out that they were looking for a spot to build a nursery. For their theme they chose straw and twigs, and the building site they selected was our white wicker cabinet that sat, adorned with my frog collection on its shelves, under the covered portion of our patio.

The nest left a lot to be desired in its construction, but after a couple of days of sitting and waiting, a tiny pinkish tinged egg appeared. Two days later, another egg lay beside the first one, and "Cooey" and "Mr. Gray" took turns patiently sitting on the nest day and night. At first, they flew away each time we opened the door to the patio/nursery, but after a week, they became accustomed to us and allowed us to come close enough to take a picture.

Watching them became a source of great pleasure and interest, so I decided to learn more about doves, as I had never been so closely involved with them before. We were surrogate grandparents it seemed. From their colors and markings, I determined they were mourning doves, so named for their low toned moaning "cooah, coo, coo, coo," which sounded so sweet and yet mournful. The nest that appeared so inadequate and flimsy to us was typical of their species, and the two egg family was also average for them.

We decided not to put food out for them, but to let them have their meals "out" as they seemed very healthy, robust, and capable of finding their favorite food without human intervention. I don't know if "Cooey" had any late night cravings for chocolate covered mealworms, but we certainly had no desire to search them out for her, and left that up to "Mr. Gray."

Although it rained hard and the March winds blew strongly, the fragile little nest was well protected from the elements, and its precious contents were safe for the required 12- to 19-day incubation period.

I was saddened to learn that these lovely birds don't often live much longer than a year, but it was interesting to note that they produce many offspring to insure the continuation of the species. "Cooey" and "Mr. Gray" were going to be a very busy couple it would seem.

After several conversations with both of them, we all agreed that we should come up with suitable names for the babies-to-be. Because we didn't know the sexes of either baby bird, we chose "Lovey" and "Dovey" as appropriately genderless names with strong family history attached, and we quickly ruled out "Hunter."

The mourning doves made their appearance into our lives at a time of personal family tragedy, so we realized that they brought with them a message of new life and God's plan for the continuation of lovely things in His world. It was not mere coincidence that this symbol of the Holy Spirit, the dove, flew down to bring us some degree of comfort and assurance.

We lost our 41-year-old nephew suddenly the same day that "Cooey" laid the first egg in the nest, and as we mourn his untimely death, we watch these birds and understand that he is a peace with the Lord. Although his life was short, the good and precious memories of him will forever remain in our hearts and memories.

May 10, 2010

IRREPLACEABLE LOSSES

My heart is filled with grief as I write this, but it is something that I must do to begin the long process of healing from an unthinkable tragedy. On Sunday, May 2, Nashville was deluged with rain of biblical proportions, and flooding occurred in many areas of our city. Waters from the Cumberland and Harpeth rivers exceeded their boundaries, and creeks all over town turned into raging streams, destroying and enveloping anything within miles of them.

My 88-year-old father and his 78 year old wife, unaware of the seriousness of the situation, got into his truck and started out of his condominium complex onto the main road, which was partially covered with rushing water. Despite shouts from bystanders for him not to proceed any further, his hearing loss and stubborn determination prevented him from heeding their warnings. By the time he realized that the water was too deep and the current too swift, his truck was swept under the raging waters, trapping both of them inside. We have spoken with eyewitnesses on the scene who told us of the heroic attempts of a young man who nearly lost his own life in a valiant effort to save theirs. We pray for him and ask God to bless him for his actions.

We had just left town early that morning, headed for a week-long vacation at the beach, and I spoke with my father mid-morning from my cell phone. I cautioned him not to leave the house because of the heavy rains and predictions of some flash flooding. By the time neighbors started calling us with reports of heavy flooding in our area, I was unable to reach Daddy by phone and had friends and family members trying to locate him, thinking he was evacuated to a shelter with others. One of our sons heard on the evening news that an unidentified elderly couple had lost their lives when their truck was submerged in high waters. He called the hospital, gave them my father's name, and was told only that he was in the ER there. Upon arrival, he learned that both of them were deceased, and I was called with that tragic news.

We drove all night to get back home, and could not absorb the reality of what had happened. The last image of my Daddy was the day before we left, when we went to visit and leave him a list of contact phone numbers for our sons in case he needed something while we were gone. He was busy painting little yard art statues for their patio, which was so typical of him. He always had a project of some kind going on. Before we left, I kissed him on his forehead and told him we would see him in a week, and I would call when we got to our destination so he wouldn't worry.

My mother and father married at the age of 18, and 10 months later, the day before his 19th birthday, I was born. He had saved coins in a jar for the duration of the pregnancy, and paid the hospital bill with his savings. A dark, curly-headed Italian boy who worked hard and arose before daybreak every morning to work with his father and two brothers in the family produce business, he was a bit of a rebel and always headstrong, but faithful and loyal to his wife and daughter. When I was 11 years old, and hoping for a baby sister, I got a baby brother, who quickly became the blessing that made our family complete.

Daddy served in World War II as an aircraft mechanic, and after the war, he obtained his own pilot's license and small plane. His ultimate goal was to teach me to fly as well, but my mother put her foot down on that plan very quickly. He loved to build things and tinkered with engines constantly. He loved to fish, and always liked being on the water. He and his brother bought a little fishing boat together, and from there, he acquired a small runabout which became the first in a series of boats he owned and enjoyed throughout his life.

Some of his happiest moments were spent at the dock where their boat was tethered, with my mother and their many friends. When Mamma died at the age of 59, his world crumbled and he grieved for such a long time. Three years after her death, he remarried and found companionship once more that lasted for 26 years, until the day they died together in that tragic accident.

The tragedy that claimed the life of my father and his wife is the kind of thing I used to see on the news, never imagining in my worst nightmares that something of that nature could happen to someone I loved. The days and weeks that followed were unbelievably difficult, and I know that it was only through God's grace, the many prayers, countless acts of kindness by others, and the love and support of family and friends that we were able to somehow endure our unspeakable loss. Taking one day at a time proved to be too much, so I had to try one hour at a time and even that seemed overwhelming at times.

Treasure every moment with those you love for we never know when it might be the last time together.

CPSIA information can be obtained
at www.ICGtesting.com
Printed in the USA
FFOW02n1348110318
45629608-46460FF